Happy Birthday

for Kirstine

from Walter

June 2021

NATURAL MANDALAS

NATURAL MANDALAS

30 NEW MEDITATIONS TO HELP YOU
FIND PEACE AND AWARENESS IN THE
BEAUTY OF NATURE

LISA TENZIN-DOLMA

DUNCAN BAIRD PUBLISHERS

LONDON

Natural Mandalas

Lisa Tenzin-Dolma

First published in the United Kingdom and Ireland in 2006 by
Duncan Baird Publishers Ltd
Sixth Floor, Castle House
75–76 Wells Street
London W1T 3QH

Conceived, created and designed by Duncan Baird Publishers

Managing Designer: Manisha Patel
Designer: Justin Ford
Editor: James Hodgson
Commissioned artwork: Christopher Gibbs

British Library Cataloguing-in-Publication Data:
A CIP record for this book is available from the British Library

ISBN-10: 1-84483-229-5
ISBN-13: 9-781844-832293

1 3 5 7 9 10 8 6 4 2

Typeset in Mrs Eaves
Colour reproduction by Colourscan, Singapore
Printed in Singapore by Imago

Publisher's note: This book does not recommend meditation with mandalas for the specific treatment of any disability, only for the enhancement of general well-being. Meditation is beneficial for most people and generally harmless, but those unsure of its suitability for them should consult a medical practitioner before attempting any of the meditations in this book. Neither the publisher nor the author can accept responsibility for any injuries or damage incurred as a result of following the meditations in this book, or using any of the meditation techniques that are mentioned herein.

"A mandala is a pattern or device on which to meditate. ... By absorbing the mandala into his or her own consciousness, the meditator re-orientates their world-view, as their inner focus shifts from the distractions of the outer world to the virtues of self-awareness, wisdom and compassion.

Nature, the creative life-force, is in many ways the ultimate mandala. ... Natural mandalas can be seen wherever we choose to look. The whorl of a shell, the tightly furled petals of a rose, the age-rings within the trunk of a tree, the patterns made by leaves against the sky — all of these, and more, are portals to a realm that transcends the mundane."

CONTENTS

INTRODUCTION

MANDALAS — THE SYMBOLIC PICTURES USED IN MEDITATION —
TRADITIONALLY DEPICT THE DIVINE ARCHITECTURE OF THE COSMOS.
HOWEVER, SYMBOLS OF NATURE CAN BE AN APT SUBJECT FOR MODERN-
DAY MANDALAS. THROUGH NATURE WE RECONNECT WITH ESSENTIAL
EXPERIENCES OF SELF-AWARENESS, SIMPLICITY AND PEACE.

A mandala is a pattern or device on which to meditate. The term is especially associated with the elaborate designs used for meditation in the Tantric Buddhist tradition of Tibet — complex hierarchies of imagery within a circular frame, charged with a symbolism that invariably strikes modern-day Westerners as profoundly esoteric. Essentially these devices represent the palace of the gods, in countless variations. By absorbing the palace of the mandala into his or her own consciousness, the meditator re-orientates their world-view, as their inner focus shifts from the distractions of the outer world to the virtues of self-awareness, wisdom and compassion.

Modern mandalas are often designed to be more accessible to today's seekers, thanks to a broader repertoire of symbolism — for example, such

Left: The moon makes a compelling mandala — thanks to not only its circular shape but also its dark side and its intrinsic unworldliness.

motifs as the Celtic endless knot, which represents the perpetual flow of time and the journey of the pilgrim; and the mud-transcending lotus, suggestive of pure, undefiled spirit.

Nature, the creative life-force, is in many ways the ultimate mandala. The Tantric mandalas of Buddhism depict the elements and the cycle of birth, life and death — both primal forces of nature — together with various deities and demons. Such devices were carefully designed by sages to open up the seeker's perceptions. However, it is possible to achieve a similar effect using nature's actual phenomena as an object of meditation. Nature's symbolism is apparently simple yet in many ways profoundly intricate. By dwelling on the vast interconnectedness of all living things we can access important insights.

In nature, mandalas can be seen wherever we choose to look. The whorl of a shell, the tightly furled petals of a rose, the age-rings within the trunk of a tree, the patterns made by leaves against the sky — all of these, and more, are portals to a realm that transcends the mundane. Each object of focus becomes a symbol, opening up the mind to a greater understanding of life. We attain a deep knowledge of our place in the grand scheme of the cosmos — a knowledge that is intuitive rather than intellectual. We perceive ourselves as a single strand in the web of life, yet paradoxically this gives us an experience of unity.

We know ourselves to be both the weaver and the web. The sense of separation that is the cause of so many of humanity's problems is dissolved by the understanding that we are a single cell in the body of life itself, nurtured and supported in our growth, and capable of fully realizing our potential.

MANDALAS AND MEDITATION

The origins of the mandala tradition can perhaps be dated back to the cave drawings and rock inscriptions created by our primitive ancestors, as a source or reflection of spiritual energy. A mandala is a sacred image which, when we focus on it, draws our attention inward and enables us to understand its symbolic meaning and absorb this into the mind. The symbols of a mandala are set within a geometric or symmetrical pattern, and the resulting image serves to express different elements of our deep self, the "inner me" beneath our surface personality. Whereas the conscious mind uses words to categorize and define both objects and experiences, the unconscious mind deals in images and symbols, which generate various kinds of sensations and perceptions. When we attune ourselves to a mandala, with the right kind of concentration, we experience a change in consciousness. Meditating on a mandala takes us on a journey into our wise centre which is in harmony with the cosmos.

The shape considered to be most potent in a mandala is the circle. This is used in all mandalas, and other shapes such as the square and triangle are secondary to it. The circle represents the endless cycle of life, with no beginning and no end. The space within the circle symbolizes the inner realm, a magical space enclosed and protected by the periphery. The still, central point from which the circumference is measured represents the self, the spiritual hub that drives the wheel of life in perpetual motion.

In nature the circle can be found in the sun, the moon and the planets. It is the defining shape of fruits such as oranges and cherries. It gazes back at us through the iris and pupil of the eye. It can also be seen in the centre of a flower, and the head of a mushroom. Meditating on the circle in nature's mandalas can bring us to a realization of wholeness, harmony and inner peace.

A variation on the circle is the spiral, in which the circular motion uncoils like a spring. Instead of converging on a closed meeting point, each section moves on to a new phase, reminding us of the progression of understanding that ultimately leads to true knowledge – the deep spiritual self. Then there is the oval, which like the circle is enclosed, and is a symbol of birth and renewal. These are all important shapes in nature. The square, by contrast, symbolizes containment: it creates a sense of solidity and security which "holds" the energy of the symbols placed within it. All the shapes within a mandala help to enhance the power of its individual symbols, and bring about an expansion of consciousness when we meditate on them.

Meditation on a mandala involves a process of relaxation. Initially your mind may be tempted to focus on separate aspects of the mandala, and to try to decipher what the symbolism means to you personally. The natural mandalas in this book are accompanied by a kind of "pre-meditation" tour of their symbolism, to acquaint you with some of the thinking that has determined the visual details. However, when meditating in the true sense of the word, it is important that you step out of your "monkey mind", which seeks constant stimulation and distraction, and just let the mandala make an impression on your awareness without trying to analyze it. Your intellectual faculties should not be engaged. All you are doing is absorbing the imagery and allowing it to make its own impact on your consciousness, without wilful interference.

The aim of meditation is to quieten your mind. Within the stillness that arises from this is found a sense of deep tranquillity and harmony that gradually becomes the basis for your outward experiences and self-expression. The nature of your everyday surface mind is movement: thoughts constantly come and go, hopping from one subject to another, in a way that is liable to draw you away from your purpose. When you meditate on a mandala, these peripheral thoughts can pull you away at first, but with practice you can allow them to roam in the background, without following them through. If you strain to avoid thinking, your thoughts will take control; but if you relax and merely allow them to chatter without giving them your attention, they will settle down and become less of a distraction. Each time your mind attempts to draw you away from your meditation, gently bring your focus back to the mandala.

Mandalas are such a powerful tool for meditation because the mind creates its strongest associations through imagery. If you think of a flower, or ripples in a pond, or a constellation, an image will immediately arise in your mind. Being intensely visual, and framed within a dynamic design, a mandala, once absorbed into your mind, works changes on your mental state, which then filter through to influence your feelings. This can generate a heightened state of awareness in which insights come to the surface and your perceptions are enhanced.

Your reactions to any situation or experience are fully dependent upon your perception at that particular moment. If you are feeling upset, a slight let-down can be devastating. If you are feeling strong and confident, the same disappointment will appear minor, and can be easily dismissed. Mandala meditation enables you to perceive clearly and from a state of well-being, and this sends ripples out into your approach to the ups and downs of daily life. You can discover this for yourself by meditating on the photograph of a flower, on page 17.

NATURE AS SPIRITUAL REFRESHMENT

For centuries we have felt a sense of spiritual sustenance when observing a glorious sunset, or a distant lake shore, or the gentle undulation of grasses in the wind. Our primitive ancestors no doubt had more basic feelings that we will never be able to recapture. But certainly today, contemplating nature has a healing and calming effect on the senses and the soul.

Nature as spiritual refreshment is a topic in the literature of many different cultures. In ancient Greece the philosopher Aristotle stated that "In all things of nature there is something of the marvellous." The Christian tradition tells how Jesus spent forty days and nights in the desert, wrestling with his inner demons, which culminated in his emergence as a great teacher. The German poet, scientist and thinker Johann Wolfgang von Goethe (1749–1832) considered that whenever the best was attained in human nature, this was a reflection of the beauty and wholeness of the universe. In his

continues on page 18

MEDITATE ON A FLOWER

In this meditation, the close-up photograph of a flower, opposite, functions as a mandala.

1 Find a quiet space where you will not be disturbed for five minutes, switch off the telephone, and sit comfortably on a chair or cushion with this picture of a flower at eye level, about an arm's length from you. Rest your hands in your lap, and keep your back straight but relaxed.

2 Take three deep breaths, exhaling fully each time, and then proceed to breathe normally, maintaining a steady rhythm with your in-breaths and out-breaths.

3 Rest your eyes on the image of the flower, allowing your gaze to be slightly off-focus. Avoid staring hard at the image, lest you strain your eyes. Keep your attention on the flower depicted here. Each time your thoughts pull you away, bring them gently back. Do not try to analyze or pick out details of the flower. Simply allow it to be there in your consciousness. Ultimately, there is no distinction between you and the flower. The flower is outside you, yet at the same time it is sitting within the depths of your mind.

4 After five minutes, or when you feel ready to stop, take three deep breaths, exhaling fully each time, and resume your normal breathing rhythm. Close your eyes for a moment, and wiggle your fingers and toes. Take a few minutes to absorb the feeling of stillness. Consider any insights that occur to you and, if you wish, write them down: it can be helpful to keep a journal of your experiences and perceptions.

The same approach, of course, can be taken to meditate on a real flower. The ideal choice would be a flower such as a rose or a daisy — one with either a pattern of overlapping petals or a central disk surrounded by florets. Be sure not to remove the flowerhead from the plant, as the point of meditation is to accommodate yourself to the natural world rather than vice versa.

Right: With its swirling vortex pattern, this detailed view of the centre of a sunflower draws the observer into a dynamic symmetry, making the image an ideal subject for a natural mandala meditation.

scientific writings he insists that it is not always necessary to look for reasons behind the phenomena of the natural world, that sometimes it is more appropriate simply to appreciate them for what they are. Jacob Boehme (1575–1624), a Teutonic philosopher and mystic, spoke of recognizing God in every blade of grass. The poetry of the thirteenth-century Sufi master Rumi describes the life of the spirit as being contained and expressed within all aspects of the natural world. World literature is rich in references to nature as nurturer of the soul.

Nature is refreshingly uncomplicated. Like the spirit, it transcends boundaries, and is not subject to divisions of culture or creed. A flower never wishes to be a tree: it accepts the bending wind, the nourishing sun and rain, and willingly offers its nectar to passing bees and butterflies. The rhythms of life are accepted without question by plants and animals, and so we can learn from nature a great deal about how to flow with the tides in our own lives by refusing to participate in a futile struggle against the inevitable. Anyone who tunes in to nature understands that all things are part of the flow of the universe, and have their own unique place within an overall interdependence. And because everything that exists naturally is an expression of the sacred, in nature we recognize an infinite power.

Of course, the other key factor that links nature with inner refreshment lies in the contrast between nature and society: nature can be a way of seclusion, a place to be alone. In the East, especially in China and Tibet, monasteries are frequently sited in remote areas, high in the mountains. This allows the seeker of spiritual truths to be set apart from the everyday dramas of non-secular life. Living quietly and peacefully, with respect for the environment and its gifts and challenges, we can purify our minds, allowing the spiritual self to shine through. Many small, self-sustaining communities, based on values of harmony with nature, downsizing and charitable involvement with local people, attest to the appeal of this idea.

Yet, of course, the experience of tranquil seclusion in nature can often be obtained without distancing oneself too much from normal, social routines. You can sit in the countryside and watch nature astir around you — worms making their air-tunnels, insects helping plants to pollinate, birds prospecting twigs for their nests, depending on the time of year. Or you can sit by a river, a lake or the sea, and watch the flow of water, the stuff of life. For a more awe-inspiring view you can lie on the ground on a clear night and observe the overhead procession of the stars. Refreshment for the spirit is all around us, and even city-dwellers may find it readily in a park or garden.

NATURE AS PURE BEING

Nature expresses the pure and harmonious state of being that is sought through meditation. In the process of accepting ourselves as we are in nature, we become aware of the simple progression of birth, death and regeneration that is present in all forms of life on our planet. This awareness brings with it a profound sense of spiritual connection. The dualities of good and bad, appetite and reason, that the eighteenth-century French philosopher Jean-Jacques Rousseau considered to be the result of humanity's development from

STONE CIRCLES

One of the deepest connections humankind can make with nature is to tune in to the dynamic energies or force-fields that lie within the Earth. In various different cultures, from Native North American to Celtic European, certain areas of landscape have been seen as reservoirs of power – places where the forces of nature are especially concentrated and potent.

Understanding this, our distant ancestors erected standing stones, dolmens and stone circles to harness this natural energy, which they then used in spiritual ceremonies aimed at strengthening and unifying the tribe.

It would not stretch credulity too far to suggest that prehistoric stone circles are three-dimensional mandalas placed within a landscape. When you walk among such structures, or contemplate an aerial view of their mysterious patterns (see opposite), it is impossible not to be impressed by their silent power.

Right: Stonehenge, in Wiltshire, England, is Europe's best-known stone circle, used for ceremonies linked with solar and lunar cycles. The first stones were laid by Neolithic peoples more than 5,000 years ago.

the "noble savage" to the "civilized" human being, are dissolved in the perception of all living things as an expression of spirit.

Looking at nature in the broadest perspective, we see a vast interactive system that enables the survival of life in all its forms — a great drama featuring rain and sun providing energy for growth, wind dispersing seeds, and predators ensuring a natural balance between animal species. The Gaia theory formed in the 1960s by James Lovelock views the Earth as an "intelligent", self-regulating, self-sustaining organism, constantly acting to maintain the balance necessary for survival. Just as the cells in your body each have their purpose in sustaining health, working together to create an intricate, coherent whole, so each component within nature contributes to the good of the entire organism within the complex web of life. We ourselves belong to this web, and to see this is to relish, rather than fear, our overlapping cycles of living and dying.

Nature is not only pure being, it also presents to us in infinitely various forms the *beauty* of pure being. From natural beauty we derive inspiration and inner nourishment. At its most extreme this shades into awe, convincing us of life's richness, its spiritual value. A feeling of rightness and perfection elevates us to a sense of communion with the creative force that gives rise to and lies within all these manifold forms. By attuning ourselves to this feeling, we step out of our everyday selves, becoming not merely a witness or participant, but something far more significant — a kind of natural stakeholder in beauty, in meaning, in joy.

The sense of joy, although requiring deep meditation to be fully accessed, can be felt in a more diluted way by appreciating nature outwardly in various activities. Walking or hiking, swimming, climbing, or just experiencing the breath of a breeze on naked skin, all bring about a heightening of the senses. This helps to remove the mind from the problems and distractions of everyday life, and its uncomfortable subscription to role play, power struggles, the assertion and competition of egos. Sitting in silent contemplation of a natural scene or feature enables you to pierce the wildness, to move beyond the outward forms to unity and universality, to knowledge of the simplicity of the pure intelligence that lies behind the forms, and to an understanding of infinity.

NATURE AND RELAXATION

Deep contemplation, and even more so meditation, requires conscious mental engagement. However, nature can also work more subtle effects on our state of mind, relaxing us to an experience of peace without our having to make any conscious mental efforts at all. Simply gazing at a green or rocky landscape, or looking out to an azure sea, or being aware of clouds drifting endlessly overhead while you are involved in some physical activity (anything from playing with your children to mending a fence or setting up an easel for painting), can give us a sense of natural belonging. The typical shapes found in nature, which complement each other so well, have a restful effect on the eyes and the mind. Green, of course, is a famously restful colour, valued by actors for their pre- or post-performance unwinding in the "green room", and the greeny blues or greys of the ocean can put us at ease in a similar way. However, the reds, browns and ochres of a desert can be no less soothing in the right light.

NATURE AND INSPIRATION

Many people have chosen to surround themselves with nature to nourish their best thoughts. Carl Gustav Jung (1875–1961), the Swiss-German psychiatrist whose ideas opened up the landscape of the mind and illuminated knowledge of the inner life, was a champion of nature's healing power. Jung insisted on living near water, which he considered to be a symbol of the collective unconscious and of intuitive wisdom. He was deeply influenced by the Romantic poetry of Blake, Wordsworth, Coleridge and Goethe, all of whom wrote of the soul's need for the beauty of the natural world. Typically, according to the Romantic world-view, there is no separation between nature and spirit.

However, this deep affinity was appreciated long before the nineteenth century. The sixth-century BC Chinese philosopher Lao Tzu, whose *Tao Te Ching* has inspired so many people, linked the natural world to human attributes, and wrote his stanzas as instructions for right living. He wrote about the Tao, the mysterious, all-pervasive life-force. By attuning to nature, it is possible to perceive this life-force flowing through nature's many forms. "The highest good is like water," he wrote. "Water gives life to the ten thousand things and does not strive. It flows in places men reject, and so is like the Tao."

CALMING WATER

In psychology, water symbolizes the unconscious mind — the thoughts, feelings, urges and memories that are buried deep within the psyche. This includes the collective unconscious, the imprinted inherited memories and archetypal patterns of generations, which form a blueprint for the "group mind" of humanity. Water has always been associated with the primordial fluid from which all living things are born. The magical elixir which in countless myths has the power to bestow immortality, bring the dead back to life, and cure all diseases, has its natural analogy in water. In Greek myth, the souls of the dead drank the waters of Lethe, a river in Hades (the underworld), to bring about forgetfulness of all that had gone before, so that they would not mourn the loved ones they had left behind. Water is also the basis of the Fountain of Youth, sought by heroes in many myths. In magic, still water in a puddle, a lake or a bowl is used for scrying (a form of divination), as it allows the mind to settle and see images from deep within the unconscious.

But quite apart from these symbolic associations, water has purely physical properties that make it psychologically important to us. If you sit by a lake on a still day, the perfect flatness of the surface of the water has a soothing effect, helping to slow the mind into a state of meditative calmness. Watch a fish come to the surface, or cast a stone into the water. Ripples will radiate in an outward flow, creating circles within circles — a natural mandala revealing how stillness can accommodate motion and change. At the same time, the reflections of clouds or the surrounding landscape on the water's surface create dreamlike images that can draw the mind inward.

A river embodies the flow of the life-force, swirling around obstacles, creating a complex pattern of eddies and currents. It moves inexorably from its source to the sea. The mind shares this compulsion to integrate, being drawn toward unifying the diverse parts of ourselves with the greater whole. The sounds of moving water are relaxing and hypnotic, so it is not surprising that meditation music often includes the murmur of a stream or river.

THE LIVING FOREST

We have explored some of the universal and cultural associations of water, which come into play in some of the natural mandalas in this book. By contrast to water's essential simplicity, the forest is a complex network of interdependent life forms — but still rich in meaning for the meditator. The quality of light in a forest is soft and diffused, often with dappled shade where the sun's rays play through foliage. This greenish light coupled with a hushed stillness can almost make you feel you are underwater. Yet, if you listen, the forest is not silent. Sounds of rustling foliage, snuffles and squeaks of small creatures, and high-pitched bird calls all form part of the sensory experience. The rich scent of leaves and bark, earth and loam, awakens the olfactory sense, releasing memories and recalling associated emotions. All of these factors combine to create an ever-changing three-dimensional mandala that takes the mind away from its routine chatter. The forest embodies shelter or refuge, yet it also holds an atmosphere of mystery that enables you to attune yourself more clearly to the infinite mystery of the spiritual self.

Hermits and sages in many spiritual stories have retreated to the forest to experience the simplicity of living in the wild. Within the forest can be found all that is needed to sustain life: shelter, fuel, food. In the deciduous forest nature's cycles are easily seen. By meditating on, say, a forest leaf or an acorn we can open up a pathway that leads to our own still centre.

CLOUDS AND THOUGHTS

The sky is our gateway to the infinite spaces of the universe. At a human level, it can be likened to the vast, unexplored areas of the mind. By extension, the clouds are like our thoughts, which arise, drift across the field of view, join with others and then dissolve into the boundless silence of the spiritual self. If you look up at the sky you will feel as though you are rising into it, floating beyond the confines of your bodily self. Cloud meditation enables you to drift, light-headed, toward a heightened awareness of your place in a universe that is beyond our powers of measurement or even imagination.

Cloud formations can make interesting quasi-mandalas — whether rolling cumulus, with its soft hills and valleys; the ripples of a mackerel sky, like fish scales; wispy cirrus, like strands of silky hair in the upper strato-sphere; or dark, rain-bearing nimbostratus, which wraps us in a blanket, and reminds us that water is the source of life.

When you use clouds as a mandala, allow your awareness to drift into the formation that is your focus for meditation. Soften your vision so that the cloud becomes the centre of your awareness. Drift with it and into it, and feel yourself becoming lighter as you liberate your mind from earthly cares and concerns. Breathe gently and easily, and feel your body relax as your mind rises to meet the cloud. You may find that soon you can dissolve into the cloud and become one with it – like part of the breath of the life-force itself. If you begin to feel dizzy, or in any case when you are ready to stop meditating, draw your line of vision slowly downward to focus on the horizon.

THE MEDITATION GARDEN

A garden can be an expression of your connection with nature. Spiritual gardens may take many forms, depending on geographical factors, the purpose of the garden, and the cultural tradition it reflects. Although a garden is usually considered to be a way of taming and civilizing nature, leaving a wild area where nature is allowed to take its course can provide an appealing contrast.

SAND MANDALAS

In Buddhist Tibet, impermanent mandalas, known as *kilkhor*s, are created using flowers, dyed grains of rice, crushed precious stones and coloured grains of sand. In a spiritual ceremony called the Kalachakra Initiation, the mandala is painstakingly laid out in areas of different-coloured sands. The purpose of the ceremony is to bring about personal and world peace, and to remind each participant of the transitory nature of the material world. Afterwards, the mandala is swept away until no trace remains.

You can create your own sand mandala on a beach, close to the shore. Begin at the centre of the mandala and work outward, using your finger, a shell or a small stone to etch a symmetrical design into the sand. You can choose motifs from mandalas in this book for your sand mandala, or create your own design using geometric shapes, circles or spirals. When you have finished, sit back and meditate on your mandala. Then wait for the tide to come in and wash it away.

A garden can be planned specifically with meditation in mind. Any individual area can be laid out like a mandala – as a special place in which to celebrate the magnificent creations of nature and allow the mind to open itself up to beauty all around. Pattern can be provided in the planting scheme or in the hard surfaces – for example, an alternation of stone paving and herringbone brickwork or gravel. If you wish, you can treat the whole garden as a mandala, which you access either by sitting and meditating in it, or by

Right: This Tibetan *kilkhor* (sand mandala) is composed of intricate lines and areas of coloured sand and stone. After a short time, the patterns are swept away to represent the transient nature of life.

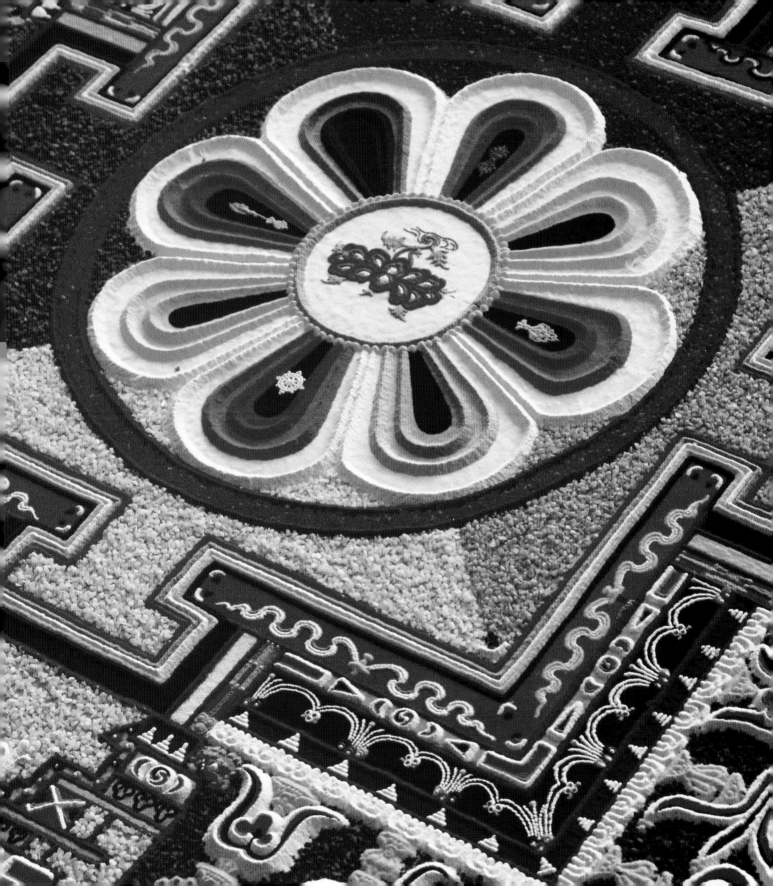

meditatively walking around a particular route. Paths, with ornaments used as punctuation points, can be planned to guide the eye. Water features will provide sound and movement.

The Zen garden, in the Japanese Buddhist tradition, is a customized meditation space. Zen gardens use "sand", which is actually crushed granite in shades of white-grey to beige. In the most common, dry-style Zen gardens, sculptured rocks are used to create mountains and islands, each one usually in the approximate shape of a tortoise or a crane — creatures known for their longevity. Bridges cross the "seas" of sand from one rocky island to another, and are pleasing to the eye. Ornaments act as focal points and help to provide a sense of perspective.

A Chinese garden is composed of an area of rocks, plants and water, surrounded by buildings and walls which provide decorative architectural structures and enhance the effect of the internal design. The organization of the Chinese garden is aimed at promoting a feeling of relaxation and well-being. It is rigorously planned to include the elements, expressed through plants, water, stones and architecture, with a balance of yin and yang in a harmonious design that employs unusual perspective and a great deal of metaphorical meaning. Instead of imitating nature, the creator of a Chinese garden manipulates the components of nature to create contrast and arouse the emotions. Traditional Chinese plants such as peonies and bamboo bring colour and texture into the garden as well as symbolic meaning.

TRANSCENDENTAL RETREAT

There is an important tradition of retreat that lies outside the history of monastic practice – a less institutionalized approach, which was especially important in America in the nineteenth century. A life lived in harmony with nature was proposed by the Boston Transcendentalists, a movement of progressive thinkers whose ideas stemmed from the theories of Immanuel Kant (1724–1804) and the German Transcendentalists. The Boston movement extolled the gifts and beauty of the natural world, rejected new technology, and aimed to create a new form of literature based on humankind's relationship with nature. They were educated people who chose to identify themselves with the harmony and simplicity of the natural world, and to adopt a different perspective on spirituality, religion, art and politics from that provided by the general social mores of their time. The Transcendental Club was formed in Boston, Massachusetts, in 1836, and attracted a growing number of writers and intellectuals. Ralph Waldo Emerson, who hosted the meetings, gave a succinct summary of the credo: "Nature is loved by what is best in us." Henry David Thoreau, Margaret Fuller, Bronson Alcott and his daughter Louisa May Alcott, and William Ellery Channing the younger, are the best-known members, and lived near Boston, in Concord. Of these, Emerson was the most celebrated during his lifetime, although Thoreau's work is now of equal renown, and he is hailed as America's first environmentalist.

Emerson offered Thoreau a plot of land at Walden Pond, less than two miles from Concord, and there he lived on and off for two years in a cabin built with his own hands. In his book, *Walden*, Thoreau described his experiences through the changing seasons, and put forward his ideas about living close to nature, retreating from the world and rejecting the superficialities of civilization. The purpose of this experimental retreat was to live fully attuned to the natural world, and to drink deep of the bounty of nature, while also refraining from leaving an indelible impression on the landscape.

The Transcendentalists, whose values stemmed from the ideal of living in harmony with the natural world, by extension campaigned for a just balance in society, the abolition of slavery, and rights for women. Combining mysticism and philosophy, they promoted the supremacy of intuition over reason, with nature as an inspiration and guide to the life of the spirit. The influence of the Transcendentalists has been pronounced: many modern-day communes, with their various degrees of eco-consciousness, owe a great deal — even indirectly — to the ideas of Emerson, Thoreau and their collaborators.

The mandalas in this book draw upon traditional symbolism associated in various cultures with different natural features, the most important of which are profiled below.

TREES

Trees are powerful conduits for life-energy on our planet. They process carbon dioxide into oxygen so that we can breathe; the humus from their decaying leaves enriches the ground; and they also provide habitats for birds, animals and insects. Rain forests are essential for the planet's rainfall, which of course is the source of our drinking water. Myths involving trees are abundant, and some of us still "touch wood" for good luck.

In Druid lore, each tree has its own personality and symbol, and governs a month of the year. The Druids' alphabet, known as "ogham", consisted of

25 characters, each encoding an aspect of tree wisdom. Groves were considered to be natural temples — places of meditation, contemplation, wisdom and healing. Entering a grove or wood, with its diversity of trees and plant life, the Druid could associate each tree and plant with many different signifiers — a number, a month, a deity, a colour, a star, an animal and a mineral. These associations could enable a kind of cross-pollination of the mind and the senses, as well as providing a workable memory system. To the Druids and nature-worshippers all trees are sacred, and each has a specific symbolism.

There is also a great deal of tree lore outside the Western tradition. To take just one notable example, pine trees in the Far East symbolize longevity, purity, health and abundance. Like the cedar, the pine was linked with incorruptibility and tended to be planted around Chinese graves. From its resin came the mushrooms upon which Taoist immortals fed. The box, opposite, gives examples of common trees and their symbolism in different cultures.

Trees, which embody the connection between the different layers of the cosmos, make fascinating natural mandalas. Their roots are anchored deep in the ground, and often spread to encompass the same breadth of soil that their branches take up in the sky. The roots symbolize the deep self, our constant source of nourishment, while the trunk is the conduit for the life-force, the

TREE LORE

Cultures from all ages and all parts of the world have ascribed symbolic associations to different species of tree.

Almond Divine light (Biblical lands).

Apple Marriage, fertility, good health (Europe).

Birch A benevolent, protective tree in northern Europe. Used as the central pole in a shamanic yurt (tent) in Mongolia and Siberia to symbolize our ascent to the spirit world.

Cedar Tree of life (Sumeria), representing power and immortality.

Cypress Symbolizes death and mourning in the West, but longevity and immortality in the East.

Fig The sacred tree in many regions, with associations of fertility. In Buddhism, a symbol of moral teaching and immortality (the Buddha achieved enlightenment beneath a Bodhi fig).

Hazel Wisdom, prophecy (northern Europe). Eating hazelnuts is said to open the mind, and the twigs are used for dowsing.

Oak Nobility, endurance (the West). An axial symbol of male potency and wisdom in Druid lore, though with feminine associations too.

Olive Peace, joy, victory, plenty, purity, immortality, virginity (Greece, Biblical lands).

Palm The Tree of Life in Egypt and Arabia, associated with the sun as well as fertility.

Peach Immortality, longevity, spring, youth, marriage, protective magic (the East). The blossom represents virginity in Taoist symbolism.

Pine Immortality or longevity (the East). In a pair, marital fidelity (China and Japan). The pine cone is a symbol of masculine strength.

Willow A lunar and feminine symbol (China), and a Taoist image of strength in flexibility. The Tree of Life in Tibet.

Yew Death and rebirth (Europe). Commonly planted in churchyards, it straddles the everyday world and the Otherworld inhabited by the spirits of the dead. Spears and shields were made from yew, for its magical properties.

A TREE MEDITATION

This meditation is one to be performed outside, in front of your chosen tree. If possible, select a tree according to the symbolism that has particular meaning for you at this time (see box, page 37). If you wish to focus on flexibility, opt for a willow tree. For kindness and protection, a birch tree. To focus on divinatory skills or altered states of awareness, a hazel. For strength and endurance, an oak.

1 Go right up close to the tree. Touch the bark: feel its texture and observe its markings. Examine the leaves, and the blossoms or fruit, if there are any, and allow the shapes, colours and patterns to become imprinted on your mind.

2 Find a comfortable place where you can sit facing the tree, with a view of the trunk and branches. Close your eyes for a moment, and visualize the tree. Imagine that it has a message for you. (Native peoples believe that each tree is inhabited by a spirit, and you can ask for advice or guidance which will be given if you are open and receptive.) Take three deep breaths, then breathe normally.

3 Open your eyes and really look at the tree. See it as an entire organism, an eco-system for numerous life-forms. Observe how the branches spread out, the lattice they make, the way they filter the light. Draw your attention to the trunk, and focus on any prominent curves and knots. Think of the tree standing for a lifetime that is longer than your own. Look at the visible roots, and imagine them drawing nutrients and water up from the ground.

4 Absorb the image of the whole tree into your mind, and experience it there — outside you, yet inside you simultaneously. Feel the special symbolic qualities of this species absorbing themselves into your being, like water and nutrients through the tree's roots.

5 When you have finished your meditation and are ready to leave, give thanks to the tree.

body, which the roots sustain. The branches, with their leaves, flowers and fruit, represent the blossoming of potential into full fruition, and act as antennae for cosmic energy. By meditating on a tree (see box, opposite) you can strengthen your sense of wholeness and integrity, at the same time as drawing upon the symbolic resonance of your chosen tree.

THE ELEMENTS

In Western society we tend to consider only four elements: earth, air, fire and water. In Greek culture, Aristotle (384–322 BC) attributed properties to each of these elements: earth was cold and dry; water, cold and wet; fire, hot and dry; and air, hot and wet. These four elements were encapsulated within a fifth – aether or quintessence; Buddhists also speak of this fifth element. In China, the elements are wood, fire, earth, metal and water. All the elements, of course, are vital components of life, held in a perfect balance.

You can view the elements as aspects of your internal nature, as well as external forces. Earth is the element that relates to physicality, health, material possessions and work. Psychologically the earth element keeps you grounded and brings about a sense of stability and security. Air is associated with mind, thought and intellect, as well as with communication, because air is a vehicle for sound. Water symbolizes emotion, with its propensity to flow, and to change the terrain that it encounters, while taking the shape of the container that holds it. Fire symbolizes passion and inspiration, and in its ability to transmute one substance into another it can be damaging, purifying or alchemically transformative.

The symbolism of the elements is used in Eastern healing traditions, as well as in divinatory systems such as Tarot, Kabbalah, I Ching and astrology. By meditating on the elements, you can attune to their symbolic meaning

MEDITATING ON THE ELEMENTS

Working with the elements is a form of alchemy. The Greek philosophers postulated that all matter was composed of various blends of earth, air, fire and water. Thus, all substances could be transmuted into each other by creating a mixture, and varying the proportions of the elements accordingly. From c. 300 BC to c. 1500 AD this theory provided the basis for alchemical study — including the quest for the mysterious "philosopher's stone", which was believed to convert base metals into gold and, when put in wine, to create a health-restoring elixir of life.

In meditations on the elements, the base components in medieval alchemy can be likened to thoughts and desires that rest on the surface and distract you from your true purpose. The purification of these through the alchemy of meditation leads to the "gold" of wisdom and insight that brings you into contact with your essential self.

within your psyche, and use this to effect inner transformation, or bring a sense of ease and calm, or even improve health. You can choose to focus on aspects of yourself or situations in your life that need a boost. If you feel lacking in inspiration, you might choose to meditate on fire in the form of blazing logs or a candle. Meditation on a stream, a river or the sea can help you to attune to your emotions, and can enhance your intuitive faculties. If you wish to feel more grounded and practical, you can reconnect with the earth element by meditating outside in your garden, or out in the countryside. Watching the sky can put you in touch with the air element within yourself, and help you to open yourself to new horizons in your life. Even staying indoors, you can still meditate on the elements using a bowl of earth or a crystal, a glass of water, a candle and, to represent air, some incense.

The "elements" is also a term commonly used for the weather, which can be an inspiring natural mandala. Watch a storm move across the sky, and be awed by its power and intensity. Allow all your senses to become involved in this dramatic expression of natural power. Less stirring, but no less beautiful, is the whispering or roaring of the wind in the trees or blowing across water, the light rain that taps rhythms on a window, or the play of sunlight across a landscape. These can also be subjects for a mandala meditation.

THE NIGHT SKY

The sky has long been a focal point for myths and legends, and the setting for stories of deities and heroes of all cultures. Probably since our earliest ancestors gazed aloft, the sun, moon and stars have been objects of worship. In ancient Egypt the Milky Way was considered to be the cosmic milk which flowed from the breasts of Isis, the Great Mother. The Greeks thought of the sun as Apollo, the sun god, who rode his fiery chariot across the sky each day and retreated to the magical land of Hyperborea ("beyond the north wind") each year for the three months of winter.

Our solar system is situated on an arm of the spiralling Milky Way galaxy, which can be seen as a hazy band of white light across the celestial sphere, appearing brightest near the constellation Sagittarius, which points the way to the galactic centre. The galaxy is vast — if you could travel at the speed of light, it would take around 250,000 years to circumnavigate the Milky Way.

Symbolically the sun represents the spirit, the all-seeing eye of the self. Psychologically, it signifies growth and creativity, and is associated with the conscious mind and its capacity for discernment and evaluation. The moon symbolizes intuition, dreams, and the feeling or feminine self. Traditionally, farmers considered the new moon to be an auspicious time to sow seeds.

The night sky is patterned with dozens of constellations and thousands of individual stars. Many of the constellations, like Orion, Taurus and Ursa Major, are easy to recognize, and even the more prominent planets, such as Venus and Jupiter, should not present any difficulties. At sunrise and sunset you can see the planet Venus, which looks like a lone bright star, low above the horizon near the point where the sun rises or sets. Jupiter, when visible, is simply the largest, brightest object in the night sky apart from the moon. The Plough or Big Dipper, which is part of Ursa Major (the Great Bear), is the most easily recognizable of the constellations. In Greek myth, the great god Zeus fell in love with Callisto, a huntress, whereupon his jealous wife, the goddess Hera, turned her into a bear. Callisto's son, Arcturus, was about to kill the bear, unaware that this was his mother, but Zeus quickly intervened, changed Arcturus into a smaller bear, and threw mother and son into the sky, where they remain to this day as Ursa Major and Minor. As these two constellations rotate around Polaris, the pole star, which approximates to true north, every 24 hours, sailors could use astronomical observation to ascertain time as well as north's direction. All these associations can be used as material for an absorbing open-air meditation for those living in the northern hemisphere when the night sky is clear.

HALF-MOON MEDITATION

This is an ideal meditation for city dwellers who, because of light pollution, cannot see the night sky clearly. When the moon is in its middle phase, the surface features are more clearly visible than they are on the full moon.

1 Use the moon-phase data in your diary to work out roughly the best day for a half-moon meditation. Obviously a certain amount of luck will be needed, as cloud cover would spoil the effect —

though just a few clouds passing over the moon can be incorporated into your meditation.

2 Find as peaceful a place as you can, and look up at the half-moon. Try to make out as many details as possible — ridges, craters and clouds.

3 Imagine that there is someone on the moon, gazing at the Earth. Sense your connection with all living beings throughout the universe.

4 Say goodbye to your distant friend and return your attention to the Earth.

Meditating on the constellations can help you to stretch your imagination by attuning to the relevant myths, at the same time as strengthening your awareness of the unimaginably vast spaces contained within just a tiny portion of the universe. Remember that, in the midst of all this vastness, there is a place for you, and that your life interconnects with the whole. Everything that exists is composed of the stuff of stars. We are, in truth, formed from the same elements as the sun, moon and stars — elements that came into being just moments after the birth of the universe.

LEARNING FROM WATER

Water is a gentle guide to what Taoists and Buddhists term "right living". In the story of Siddhartha, the Indian prince who became the Buddha when he meditated beneath a Bodhi tree, an old boatman offered inspiration and deep understanding. His name was Vasudeva. He had spent all his life ferrying travellers across the river, and was attuned to its many moods and voices. Vasudeva gently suggested that Siddhartha pay attention to the water, and Siddhartha became aware of the faces and voices of all the people he loved, as they merged with the greater whole. He realized that the river was the river of life, travelled by all beings, who sang out their yearnings, sufferings and joys as the river held them within its embrace. The water raced toward its goal, the sea, joined by other rivers from all sides; and the water rose as steam and fell from the clouds as rain. This deeply felt perception enabled Siddhartha to experience unity, or *nirvana*. (See page 98 for the Taoist interpretation of the river, which concentrates less on unity and more on acceptance.)

The natural aim of a river is to flow to the sea, and this can be viewed as a metaphor for our deep need to connect with the spiritual source. The process of meditation has been likened to diving into an ocean of peace, with thoughts viewed as bubbles rising to the surface of the mind. If the sea suggests

maturity and experience (infinite wisdom), at the opposite extreme from this
is the spring (infinite energy). Meditating on a spring can help you to recapture the childlike, joyful aspect of yourself. A well, half-way in its symbolism
between ocean and spring, signifies the wisdom of the unconscious that can
rise, or be brought, to the surface and be used appropriately — although there
is additionally a strong connotation of mystical healing.

ANIMAL NATURE

We can learn much about ourselves from animals. Although we consider
ourselves to be special creatures, sitting comfortably at the top of the evolu-
tionary scale, our basic instincts are no different from those of many other
creatures with whom we share our planet. Like all animals, our primary urge
is survival, both individually and as a species, and our need for the compan-
ionship of the opposite sex is specifically attuned toward fulfilling this drive.
Animals are focused on living fully in the moment — something that sages constantly remind us to do in order to experience the richness of life. Our fellow
creatures give all their attention to the needs of each moment, whether this
is feeding, playing, reproducing or home-building, and are free from our
purely human anxieties about the future. Features as varied as our opposing

Right: Animals can offer rewarding subject matter for mandala meditation. The eye of this panther
chameleon from Madagascar is a particularly exotic and dramatic example.

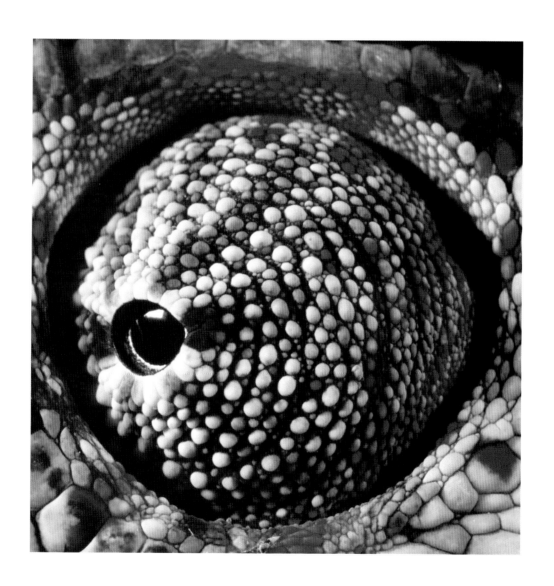

thumbs and our ability to imagine, and to write, set us apart from other creatures and have changed the face of the world, but it is important to remember that *Homo sapiens* can be guided in many ways by other animals.

Every species embodies a quality that is recognizable within human nature. By observing an animal as a mandala in motion, an expression of the energy of the created cosmos, you can intuitively discover more about the various aspects of yourself, and this leads to an increased sense of wholeness. If you pay attention, you can discover much that is useful and inspiring even within a small garden or patch of earth.

Watching ants move in an orderly line to transport food back to the nest can teach you about cooperation, the spirit of working in harmony that brings sustenance to all. The shimmering wings of a dragonfly can be seen as a message to liberate yourself from the realm of illusion, and seek your own expression of who you truly are. Following the flight of a bird across the sky reminds you of the freedom of the spirit, and can enable your mind to soar to fresh heights of imagination and inspiration. The zigzag path of swallows, the effortless hovering of a bird of prey, and the perfect formation of a flight of geese as they track the Earth's magnetic field, can raise your spirits and enable you to find solutions to problems if you are feeling confined. The proud beauty of a peacock spreading its tail, and the tiny delicacy of a hummingbird, can remind you of the magnificent beauty within yourself as well as in the world around you.

The independence of a domestic cat is a reflection of the spirit of its larger wild cousins. Observing these creatures is a study in feline grace and strength, and can remind you that there is an inherent beauty in the ability to be comfortably alone with your thoughts. The nobility of the large cats such as lions and tigers lies in their ability to create a balance between the qualities of power, strength and intent. Dogs, like their cousins the wolves, are fiercely loyal to those whom they consider to be kin, whether animal or human, and teach us about the power of faithfulness and constancy. Watch a school of dolphins and you will become immersed in a joyful sense of freedom and play, and can observe the spirit of cooperation in action. The ability of a snake to shed its skin is a message to leave the past behind, and to embrace change.

Moths and butterflies teach us about transience. The life span of an adult moth is less than a week, sometimes only a few hours. Some species of moths do not have a mouth, as they will not live for long enough to feed. Their brief existence is taken up solely with the need to perpetuate the species. Butterflies are a symbol of transformation. From the simple egg through the larval phase, through the formation of the chrysalis to the emergence of the fragile winged insect, we can learn that humble beginnings can lead to great beauty.

If you view each creature that you encounter as one of nature's intricate mandalas, you will find that your respect for the complexity of ecological balance is increased, and you will be reminded of the many facets of yourself that can be brought to bear in any circumstance. If you have a question about the most appropriate way to deal with a situation, allow your mind to wander freely, and see which animal springs to mind. Its characteristic appearance or behaviour or its symbolic meaning may give you the answer you seek.

FLOWERS

Flowers universally suggest beauty, youth and gentleness, but in many cultures they can also symbolize innocence, peace, spirituality, the transience of life or the pure bliss of paradise. Denoting nature at its peak, they could be said to compress into one telling image the whole span of birth, life, death and rebirth. Ikebana, the Japanese art of flower arranging, concentrates very much on this symbolic theme.

In botany, Compositae is the term for one of the largest families of flowering plants, encompassing many thousands of species, including the

FLOWER WISDOM

Below is a directory of flowers with the richest symbolic associations.

Anemone Transience, grief (Europe). The flower of Adonis, whom Venus transformed into an anemone

Camellia Health and fortitude (China) – though linked with sudden death in Japan.

Chrysanthemum Sun and empire, longevity and happiness (Japan). In Chinese Taoist tradition, it is associated with perfection, tranquillity and abundance – the last of these related to the fact that the chrysanthemum blooms into winter.

Heliotrope or **Sunflower** Devotion (Europe) – because the flower head follows the sun. In China this flower was the food of immortality.

Lily Purity, virginity, piety (Christianity). The Archangel Gabriel held a lily when delivering the Annunciation to the Virgin Mary. The "lily of the fields" often mentioned in the Bible is actually an anemone.

Lotus The most important flower symbol of the East – it represents spiritual growth, birth and rebirth, and creation. In Hinduism the sacred lotus grew from the navel of Vishnu as he rested on the waters, giving birth to Brahma. Buddhist gods are often depicted sitting on a lotus.

Marigold Longevity (China); the god Krishna (India); the Virgin Mary (Christianity).

Narcissus Death, sleep, rebirth (Europe).

Pansy Loving remembrance (Europe). The name comes from the French *pensée* ("thought").

Peony The imperial flower of China. Associated with wealth, glory, nobility. Sometimes described in the West as "the rose without thorns".

Poppy Sleep, dreams, sacrifice (Europe).

Rose The white rose represents innocence, purity and virginity. The red rose symbolizes passion, desire and voluptuous beauty, as well as sacrifice (the thorns suggest suffering), martyrdom, death and resurrection.

Sunflower *see* **Heliotrope**.

numerous different daisies. A single daisy flowerhead contains around 250 separate flowers, with a core of 200 disk florets (often yellow) surrounded by 50 marginal ray florets (often white). The structure of a sunflower, another member of the Compositae family, is very similar. Any daisy-like flower has a concentric symmetry that offers us a wonderful natural mandala, because when you meditate on it you can discover many worlds within the single world of the individual flowerhead — making it a profound embodiment of the multi-layered nature of existence.

Flowers, of course, unlike insects, stay still when you want them to, which means that you can readily use them, inside or outside, to perform a mandala meditation. Their aptness for this purpose is increased by the traditional symbolism that underlies many flowers (see box, page 51). In Victorian times different flowers were given specific significance in a whole repertoire of encoded meanings related to courtship, marriage and mourning. More relevant to meditation, however, is the spiritual symbolism that certain flowers have carried for thousands of years. The lotus, which has its roots in the mud and its beautiful, pristine blossoms above the surface of a lake, has long been a symbol of enlightenment — of our ability to grow through the murky elements of the material self and express the beauty of the soul in our daily lives. The rose is unusual in having secular, romantic implications as well as equally powerful evocations of the spirit — two sets of meanings that intersect with each other in the ambiguities of the word "love".

WORKING WITH THIS BOOK

Difficult though it may seem, try to resist the temptation to flick through this book, glancing at one mandala after another without really taking them in. You don't necessarily have to work with each of them in turn before moving on to the next. By all means look through the book, but bear in mind that you are not simply looking at pretty pictures. The mandalas are very much more than that. They each have a symbolic life of their own, and acquainting yourself with them will take time, just as it takes time to become familiar with new friends.

There are 30 mandalas in the book, divided into three sections: "The Fertile Earth"; "Sky, Weather and Myth" and "Animal Life". Other than that, the mandalas do not fall in any particular sequence — there is no progression, for example, from easy to difficult. Each mandala is complete in itself. There is no hierarchy between them. To guide you further in your imaginative explorations, some of the mandalas have a supplementary section, featuring evocative quotations and a paragraph expanding on an aspect of the symbolism within the image, or sometimes introducing a new image.

Some of the mandalas are drawn directly from natural observation, while others derive from symbols found in various cultures, from Japan to Celtic Europe. When selecting a new mandala on which to meditate, you can do this on a purely visual basis, choosing the one that appeals to you most at that time. Alternatively, you might consider symbolic aspects contained within the mandalas: the step-by-step text alongside each one is designed to help anyone who feels daunted by the thought of approaching the images without specific guidance (see page 57).

There may be occasions when you feel disturbed by a particular mandala. If this happens, stop your meditation. The mandala you are working with may not be the right one for you at this time. Perhaps it is too challenging or abrupt – it may be taking you too deep, too quickly. Never force yourself to persevere with a meditation that makes you feel uncomfortable. There will always be new mandalas that you can use – not only in this book, but, as we have seen, all around you in the natural world.

MANDALA MEDITATION STEP BY STEP

Meditation is at the same time disarmingly simple and challengingly difficult. Simple because the principles are readily learned, but difficult because the mind stubbornly refuses to keep to them. Meditation is not learnt in a few days. But with regular, patient practice, progress will come.

1 Find a quiet room where you won't be disturbed. Sit cross-legged on a firm cushion that raises your bottom a little way above the floor or sit in an upright chair with your feet flat on the floor – whichever you find more comfortable.

2 Place your chosen mandala at eye level about an arm's length, or slightly more, in front of you. Start with a basic pattern. If using a mandala that is not in this book, make sure that it is at least the same size as a page of this book. Straighten your back and rest your hands in your lap, fingers laced together and palms uppermost.

3 Now rest your gaze on the mandala but relax your eyes. To start with, take in the whole image, but having done so allow the eyes to rest on one point. If your eyes go into soft focus so that you can see a double image, no matter. This is better than straining your eyes. Blink only as often as necessary. Remain focused on the image. If your attention wanders, bring it back each time to the mandala. Try not to think about the mandala. Simply look at it, steadily and evenly.

To begin with, practise for five minutes each day. Remain always within the time limit in which you feel comfortable. As you become used to this form of meditation, you can extend this limit, until ultimately you may be sitting for a full 20 or 30 minutes at each session. But never rush things or push yourself too hard. Remember, the step-by-step instructions alongside each mandala are there to help you make acquaintance with the symbolism of the image in a "pre-meditation". In a mandala meditation proper, you approach the image without conscious preconceptions.

NATURAL MANDALAS

30

HOW TO USE THE GUIDELINES

The step-by-step guidelines alongside each meditation are intended

to introduce the beginner to some of the thinking behind the image

and to open the mind to some of its possible symbolic resonances.

As your meditative practice develops, these guidelines can be left

behind, so the mandalas are allowed to work at an increasingly more

intuitive and personal symbolic level. Although the mandalas are

organized theme by theme for ease of reference, your experience of

any of the mandalas is very much your own, and the thematic structure

should not be taken as definitive. All the mandalas are, at the deepest

level, a reflection of the self, the cosmos and the love

that binds everything together.

OUT OF THE ACORN

THE ACORN IS A PROVERBIAL SYMBOL OF POSSIBILITY: A CAPSULE OF FUTURE LIFE
THAT CAN BE HELD IN THE PALM OF THE HAND, IN CONTRAST TO THE MIGHTY OAK
THAT IT WILL ONE DAY BECOME. OUR OWN POTENTIAL AS CREATIVE, NURTURING
SOULS MAY SIMILARLY OUTSTRIP ALL EXPECTATIONS.

1 Look at the acorn in the centre of the mandala: a mysterious rounded egg-like form that contains all developments to come encoded within it — rather like the future that is encoded in all the innumerable events of past and present.

2 Now, turn your eyes to the fully grown tree, a parent of many acorns: the triumph of potential made actual.

3 Look next at the leaves surrounding the central square. So amazingly condensed is the acorn that every vein of every leaf of the adult tree is contained within the acorn's set of miniature biological instructions.

4 Finally, look at the circle within the square — spiritual perfection incarnated within the cosmos, like the mature oak tree incarnated within the acorn.

*Start with what you know. Mature according
to nature. Let destiny do the rest.*

CHUANG TZU (C.370–300 BC)

THE PATH OF LOVE

*"Pursue some path, however narrow and crooked,
in which you can walk with love and reverence."*

HENRY DAVID THOREAU (1817–1862)

The dark wood

The medieval Italian poet Dante began his *Inferno* with himself walking alone, lost in a dark wood (*selva oscura*) — symbolizing the confusions we can experience in our middle years. After wrong turns and encounters with wild beasts, he comes across the ghost of the poet Virgil, who

THE SELF AS TREE

"Like a tree I stand, reaching for the light, gaining strength from the darkness at my roots. My body is twisted by the storms of life, yet in my uniqueness I am beautiful."

MODERN AFFIRMATION

has come to guide him back to his path, to the nearby mountaintop. Virgil says the route will take them through Hell but that eventually they will reach Heaven, where Dante's beloved Beatrice awaits. It was Beatrice who, seeing Dante lost, sent Virgil to guide him. Apply this tale to your own life. Just how dense is the wood, and how lost are you? What are the wild beasts? Who is your Beatrice, who your Virgil? What will the view be like from the mountaintop? Reflecting on a story like this, and applying it to your own life, can enhance self-awareness.

CHERRY BLOSSOM

THE BLOSSOM OF ANY FRUIT TREE TENDS TO CLING PRECARIOUSLY AND BEAUTIFULLY TO ITS BOUGH, THEN COMES A GUST OF BREEZE AND THE BLOSSOM TREMBLES AND FALLS TO THE GROUND. THE VERY TRANSIENCE OF BLOSSOM IS WHAT MAKES IT SO PRECIOUS. NATURALLY WE SEE IN THIS A POIGNANT EMBLEM OF LIFE ITSELF.

1 Look at the square form in which the mandala sits — representing the solidity and density of the material world, as well as the constructs, mental and physical, by which we live our lives.

2 Contemplate the inner circle of the mandala, suggesting perfection and spirituality. While we live in this body, this perfection is accessible to us only by special privilege.

3 Hold the cherry blossom in your mind — it is one of many (represented by the eight smaller flowers) but is nonetheless worthy of our utmost concentration. Sense its beauty and its precariousness — its hold on the branch is uncertain.

4 Gaze into the heart of the flower. Here you see its transience and beauty coalesced into a single wonderful psalm of pure joy.

*In the cherry blossom's shade
there is no such thing as a stranger.*

KOBAYASHI ISSA (1763–1827)

Cherry viewing

The viewing of cherry blossom, while enjoying a picnic, has been a traditional celebration in Japan for almost two millennia. The blossoms, which last less than a week, are a harbinger of spring; but, of course, they are also a poignant reminder of life's transience. There are symbolic links with the samurai warrior, who, like blossom, often fell at the height of glory. Appreciation of fleeting beauties in nature can enrich everyone's year. Consider arranging a picnic around some natural climax — for example, the brief, spectacular blooming of magnolia in suburban gardens. Such an event attunes you to natural cycles and opens up your senses to the small things that matter. Organize a group meditation on your chosen phenomenon. Write haiku afterwards.

A RAIN OF BLOSSOM

"Untouchable pale petals, already saying goodbye.
Let us celebrate their parting
while welcoming the fresh spring breeze."

ANONYMOUS MODERN HAIKU, JAPAN

NATURE'S WISDOM

"Study what the pine and cherry blossom can teach.
Man is not the only keeper of enlightenment."

TAO TE CHING (4TH OR 3RD CENTURY BC)

THE RED ROSE

THE ROSE IS A MYSTICAL SYMBOL OF THE HEART, THE HUB OF THE COSMIC WHEEL.

HOWEVER, IN MANY TRADITIONS THE RED ROSE ALSO DENOTES SACRIFICE, AS THE

REDNESS CONJURES UP AN IMAGE OF BLOOD, WHILE THE BEAUTY OF THE ENFOLDED

PETALS SUGGESTS THE LOVE THAT HAS INSPIRED SUCH SELFLESSNESS.

1 Look at the square and the equal-armed cross, whose elements represent the created cosmos. Surrounding this is the circle, a symbol of spiritual perfection.

2 Imagine the intersection of the cross behind the flower, suggesting the four cardinal directions and the incarnation of spirit in the material world. The cross supports the rose, whose flowering transcends it.

3 Look at the rose within its border of surrounding leaves. The flower is both our loss and our gain: in living our lives within nature's endless cycles we experience the glorious flowering of the soul.

4 Lose yourself in the petals. The self is annihilated in the flowering of love within the heart. Take the rose into your inner self, and let it bloom in a burst of spiritual intensity.

Rose, we are your coronation ... the infinite
concordance of spirit unfolding.

RAINER MARIA RILKE (1875—1926)

NATURAL UNDERSTATEMENT

*"One of the most attractive things about
the flowers is their beautiful reserve."*

HENRY DAVID THOREAU (1817–1862)

The rose of love

The rose can be a fertile source of meditations on love, thanks to its triple symbolism — it can denote sacred, romantic and sensual love. And because the rose is also an emblem of perfection, there is a suggestion that all three types cohabit within the enlightened self, namely:

THE GIFT OF FRAGRANCE

*"The world is a rose; smell it and
pass it to your friends."*

PERSIAN PROVERB

love of and for the divine; love of a special partner with whom one chooses to make a future; and the physical love by which that future is extended, and the pleasure of the moment discovered with great intensity. Add to these the love of all beings in the cosmos and the triangle is squared. Imagine a rose both red (worldly) and white (spiritual): visualize the two hues fusing together, as a symbol of the adjusted self. Perhaps this fusion is also the sense of oneness you share with your partner, and the harmony you perceive in the cosmos.

THE CHRYSANTHEMUM

IN CHINA THE CHRYSANTHEMUM IS THE EMBLEM OF TAOIST PERFECTION, AUTUMNAL

SERENITY, FULLNESS AND LONGEVITY — WITHOUT A DOUBT BECAUSE ITS BLOOMS

CONTINUE INTO THE WINTER. THE FLOWER IS ALSO A SOLAR SYMBOL, SAID TO SERVE

AS AN INTERMEDIARY BETWEEN HEAVEN AND EARTH.

1 Look at the geometry of the mandala — the triangles and circles. The large upward-pointing triangle is masculine and symbolizes fire; the large downward-pointing triangle is feminine and denotes water. The upper part of the upward triangle has the base of the downward triangle passing through it, denoting air; the lower part of the downward triangle also has a bar across it, denoting earth. Here are all the elements.

2 Now observe the central chrysanthemum — human ingenuity has bred this flower as a pink variety, yet its natural essence remains intact, an independent being within the cosmos, subject to no human will.

3 Take this many-petalled radiance into your mind, and let it lie there as a reflection of your blossoming self, the flowering of being beyond becoming.

Life is the flower for
which love is the honey.

VICTOR HUGO (1802—1885)

A GARDEN WITHOUT WEEDS

*"Having realized his own self as the Self,
a person becomes selfless."*

UPANISHADS (C.1000 BC)

IN THE STILL DEPTHS

*"Like weary waves, thought flows upon thought,
but the still depth beneath is all thine own."*

GEORGE MACDONALD (1824–1905)

Flowers of the self

Flowers have indescribable splendour. Rooted in earth, they strive for light. They thrive best under informed, sympathetic care. All these characteristics make the flower a suitable image of the self, and readily available as an object for meditation. Imagine a particular flower as a concentration of your own qualities: for example, if you seek to nourish acceptance within yourself, think of the flower accepting all weathers — even the drought that makes it thirst and the clouds that deprive it of sunlight. By absorbing this image of the flower, and its simple interpretation, we give life to an ideal of the self — and from the image springs an energy for change. Similarly, you could focus on the hue of the flower as a positive mood or emotion — for example, red for calm assertion, or blue for enveloping sympathy.

TWO TREES FROM ONE ROOT

THERE IS A MAJOR TRADITION OF SPIRITUALITY KNOWN AS NON-DUALISM — THE
BELIEF THAT, BEHIND NATURE'S DIFFERENCES, THERE IS AN ESSENTIAL ONENESS.
THESE TWO TRUNKS FROM ONE ROOT SHOW DUALITY EMERGING FROM UNITY, YET
REMAIN TRUE TO THEIR ONENESS IN THE REALITY THAT UNDERLIES APPEARANCES.

1   Notice the contradictory perspectives in this mandala: there is no top, no bottom. The two trees inhabit a spiritual space rather than a physical space.

2   Start by looking at the four trees in the corners of the square image, outside the outer circle. This is differentiated nature. The trees belong to the same species but they are different trees, different lives.

3   Now look at the dance-like pattern of leaves within the broad brown circular band. We see the dance of nature and sense that its separate elements are connected.

4   Finally, look at the two trees joined at the roots. At the centre, where the roots are, is a *bindu* — an intense focus of energy. Lose yourself within this focus: as you do so, you realize your oneness with the cosmos.

*Wonder of wonders! This very enlightenment is the nature
of all beings, and yet they are unhappy for lack of it!*

THE BUDDHA (C.563–C.460 BC), AT THE MOMENT OF HIS AWAKENING

WAYS OF SEEING

"The tree which moves some to tears of joy is in the eyes of others only a green thing that stands in the way. Some see Nature all ridicule and deformity, and some scarce see Nature at all. But to the eyes of the man of imagination, Nature is Imagination itself."

WILLIAM BLAKE (1757—1827)

The inverted tree

Among the most potent of tree symbols is the inverted tree of Kabbalist belief and practice — that is, the mystical tradition within Judaism. This tree has its roots in the spiritual realm and grows downward to the Earth. The image symbolizes the creative potency of the spirit as

CIRCULAR MOTION

*"No matter how high the tree grows,
the leaves always return to the root."*

MALAY PROVERB

well as the notion that our lives result from the descent of spiritual energy into bodily form. Some Kabbalists use the inverted tree in meditation as a series of steps by which they ascend back toward the root — that is, toward divinity, to acquire a direct experience of God.

Essentially, the inverted tree is a living embodiment of the main Kabbalist image — the ladder of the ten *sefirot*, or the ten aspects of God. It also corresponds to a diagram of the human body, with the brain as the tree's roots. The symbol makes a rich focus for meditation.

A WORLD OF LEAVES

FROM SUCCESS AND GOOD FORTUNE TO PILGRIMAGE AND DIVINITY, THE LEAVES OF
DIFFERENT TREES SYMBOLIZE MANY THINGS IN WORLD CULTURES AND RELIGIONS.
ON A UNIVERSAL LEVEL, LEAVES CAN REPRESENT FOR US THE FLOWING LIFE-FORCE
OF NATURE, AND THE TURNING OF THE SEASONS.

1 Look at the central maple leaf — in ancient heraldry a single leaf signifies happiness. Red is the colour of fertility and energy. Feel that energy radiating through the leaf from its central stalk to its outer edges, which bound the leaf's completeness.

2 Now, visually trace the veins of the leaf outward as they radiate into the leaves in the outer circle of the mandala. This represents the individual leaf connecting with all the other leaves, and the larger organism they support and which supports them — the tree.

3 As you inhale and exhale slowly and deeply to sustain your meditation, harmonize your breathing with the leaves, as they "breathe" out oxygen into the surrounding air, thus sustaining the life of the tree, and the whole planet.

And the leaves of the tree were
for the healing of the nations.

REVELATION 22.2

TREE AFTER WIND

"The poise of a plant, the bended tree recovering itself from the strong wind, the vital resources of every vegetable and animal, are also demonstrations of the self-sufficing, and therefore self-relying soul. All history from the highest to its trivial passages is the various record of this power."

RALPH WALDO EMERSON (1808–1882)

Leaf lines

Here is a simple visualization to bring you calm when worries are nagging away at your mind. Think of a tree in an autumnal wind, all the brown and russet leaves thrashing around, often touching each other, and some of them falling to the ground. This is an image of your

REST AMIDST CHANGE

"Praise and blame, gain and loss, pleasure and sorrow come and go like the wind. To be happy, rest like a great tree in the midst of them all."

ACHAAN CHAA (DIED 1992)

many niggling anxieties. But now imagine the wind dropping, and the tree canopy gradually coming to stillness, and getting quieter by the minute. A few leaves are still fluttering down to the ground, but these are the very last. The air is now motionless, and all is calm. The tree is still majestic, still gloriously itself, despite the loss of so many of its leaves. It is now so quiet that you can hear birdsong — you recognize that this is a blackbird singing. Your anxieties have fallen away, like the leaves shed by the tree. You are at peace.

PAGODAS, POOL AND SKY

THIS MANDALA ON THE THEME OF A JAPANESE GARDEN DEPARTS FROM THE

TRADITIONAL ASSOCIATION OF GARDENS WITH GREENERY, INSTEAD DRAWING UPON

THE SYMBOLISM OF RED AS THE LIFE-PRINCIPLE. PAGODAS ARE EMBLEMATIC

MOUNTAINS, AND ALSO DENOTE THE LAYERS OF EARTH AND THE HEAVENS.

1 Look at the four pagodas around the central pool. Their upper levels represent the heavens, echoed in the blue sky. Imagine also their foundations, deep in the earth — echoed in the fiery redness of the image.

2 Turn to the pool, with its surround of sky, clouds and birds. We are simultaneously looking down from an aerial perspective and up from an earth-bound perspective.

3 At the same time we can see the decorative motifs from inside the pagodas — so that we see both their outsides and their insides, breaking down our preconceptions.

4 Finally, look at the surface of the pool, where it meets the air — an interface between two elements. The circle between pool and sky is eternity. Pass through the circle into the garden of ultimate peace.

The divine is there for all of us to see, reflected in the world's beauty, like clouds in the stillness of a lake.

JONATHAN BORGES (1872–1929)

PEONY IN A FIELD

CALLED THE "FLOWER OF TWENTY DAYS" ON ACCOUNT OF ITS BRIEF FLOWERING

SEASON, THE PEONY IS AN EASTERN SYMBOL OF WEALTH AND PROSPERITY, BUT

SHOWN AMIDST EARS OF GRAIN IT DENOTES JOY, A CONTENTED MARRIAGE,

FERTILITY — AS IN THIS MEDITATION ON DOMESTICITY.

1 Start by looking at the wheat or maize within the outer square border of this mandala. This is the domestic life we construct for ourselves by means of homes, domestic arrangements and provision of food.

2 Turn next to the four small peonies in the corners of the square — perhaps these suggest the ideals of contentment that our society wishes us to strive toward.

3 Now contemplate the central peony of the mandala, flowering among the crop. Concentrate on the central core — which is also the core of the self, from which true joy flowers. Our responsibilities — to family, friends and society as a whole — form a framework to this intense experience of inner peace, and indeed to have one without the other would cause an imbalance, a sense of something missing.

Love is infallible; it has not errors,
for all errors are the want of love.

ANDREW BONAR LAW (1858–1923)

DESTINY'S CARPET

"Once we have found the true path, destiny unfolds itself like a carpet of glorious flowers."

MODERN AFFIRMATION

The thornless rose

The peony has been described as a rose without thorns — suggesting perhaps the possibility of happiness without sacrifice. Think about this notion. Ask yourself whether true happiness can be possible without some kind of selflessness or self-denial; or perhaps it is

BUD OR BLOSSOM?

"And the day came when the risk to remain tight in a bud was more painful than the risk it took to blossom."

ANAÏS NIN (1903—1977)

selflessness that makes the thorns disappear? Or does the symbolism become more meaningful to you if the absence of thorns is associated with the absence of aggression or defensiveness? Or could the image instead suggest the idea of concealing your wounds — that is, not wearing your heart on your sleeve for all to see? Ponder an imaginary peony in this way and use it to explore your beliefs and values. Do not worry if you cannot form a set of ideas that fit harmoniously together: if necessary, place different ideas against each other as opposites.

THE LOTUS AND THE PINE

HERE IS ANOTHER MANDALA BASED ON EASTERN SYMBOLISM. THE LOTUS SUGGESTS

ENLIGHTENMENT; THE OLD PINE TREE, LONGEVITY OR OLD AGE. ENLIGHTENMENT CAN

COME AT ANY TIME. WHENEVER IT COMES, WE HAPPILY ACCEPT — NAY, EMBRACE — IN

OUR ENLIGHTENED STATE THE INEVITABILITY OF AGEING AND OF THE BODY'S DECAY.

1 First, look at the gnarled pine trees around the circular frame of the mandala, and see them as a group of people who are our contemporaries in old age — everyone mellow and beautiful with antiquity.

2 Imagine moving from the clustered pine trees to the pond in the centre of the forest. This is where the lotus of enlightenment blooms with its roots in the mud — perhaps the mud is the reality of transience, the fact that all living things have their time.

3 Look at the beautiful lotus flower and see enlightenment blossoming in your mind, in the same way that the lotus petals have opened in their watery home. Feel the unfolding of petals inside your conscious-ness as you sit with your gaze still focused on the lotus.

Do not seek to follow in the footsteps of the ancient ones; seek what they sought.

BASHO (1644—1694)

FOUR HAIKU

Autumn —
even the birds
and clouds look old.

Cormorant fishing:
how stirring,
how saddening.

Poet among pines

Basho, who lived in the seventeenth century, is Japan's most celebrated writer of the haiku, a form of short poem that captures deep truth in an observation of nature — normally with a sense of glorious evanescence as each moment passes. Basho wrote journals, combining prose

Year's end,
all corners
of this floating world, swept.

Not last night,
not this morning;
melon flowers bloomed.

BASHO (1644—1694)

and poetry, about long journeys that he made on foot through the Japanese landscape — for example, his famous account, *The Narrow Road to the Deep North*. Start your own nature diary, describing your walks in the countryside, and try interspersing your prose descriptions with haiku that capture specific observations — such as a dragonfly hovering over a stream, or the frost melting on bare branches. Each haiku should have only three short lines. Make the language as direct as you can. Be inspired by the examples above.

A DIAMOND'S LIGHT

ALL GEMSTONES BETOKEN THE GIFTS OF LIFE AND CONSCIOUSNESS — LIGHT EMERGING

MIRACULOUSLY FROM THE DARK OF THE EARTH. INDIAN ALCHEMISTS REGARDED THE

DIAMOND AS THE ULTIMATE GOAL OF THEIR PRACTICES — IMMORTALITY. TANTRIC

BUDDHISTS SAW THE DIAMOND'S HARDNESS AS ANALAGOUS TO SPIRITUAL FORCE.

1 Start by contemplating the geometric framework of this mandala — the circle symbolizing eternity and the interlocking squares symbolizing the created world. All eight points of the two squares touch the circle — when eternity is glimpsed from within the prison of time, the prison walls dissolve.

2 Now, look at the decorative framework within which the central diamond sits.

Spiritual understanding requires a gracious setting of good, loving thoughts and good, selfless actions.

3 Take the scintillating radiance of the diamond deep into your mind, and let it lie there as a reflection of your blossoming self, the flowering of being beyond becoming. Feel its spiritual force — the cutting edge of enlightenment.

*The created world is but a
small parenthesis in eternity.*

THOMAS BROWNE (1605–1682)

A GARLAND OF FLOWERS

THE TRADITION OF USING FLOWERS TO CELEBRATE ACHIEVEMENTS OR OCCASIONS
BRINGS THE NATURAL WORLD TO OUR ATTENTION, HINTS AT THE TEMPORARY STATUS
OF ALL ENDEAVOUR OR SUCCESS, AND HARNESSES NATURAL BEAUTY IN A
FRAMEWORK OF ARTISTRY. THIS MEDITATION DRAWS UPON THESE THEMES.

1 Look at the outer edges of the mandala — a square, symbolizing the created cosmos. Within the square sits a succession of circles — symbolic of spiritual perfection. Perhaps we can attain enlightenment beyond the confines of the physical?

2 Work inward toward the centre of the mandala. As you do so, dwell on each flower in turn and ask yourself what its different characteristics might symbolize; then find these qualities in yourself. With successive stages of the meditation, feel your insights becoming deeper and deeper.

3 The garland celebrates your success in moving to self-awareness. Pause at the inner circle of decorative embellishment. Beyond is a single flower, with a deep yellow centre. Pass beyond the world. Enter eternity.

*The pursuit of truth and beauty is a sphere of activity
in which we are permitted to remain children all our lives.*

ALBERT EINSTEIN (1879–1955)

DREAM WORLD

"The world is as you dream it."

SHAMANIC SAYING

An alpine flower

By conjuring up alpine flowers in a meditation, you can connect with an important truth: the fact that what might be faraway places to us could for someone else be right up close. Imagine yourself transported to a rolling green mountain landscape. All around is a panoramic

MOUNTAIN REFUGE

"Climb the mountains and get their good tidings. Nature's peace will flow into you as sunshine flows into trees. The winds will blow their own freshness into you ... while cares will drop off like autumn leaves."

JOHN MUIR (1838–1914)

wilderness. There are carpets of flowers underfoot. You notice white bog orchid, snowball saxifrage, bright magenta moss campion, and alpine buttercups. Take just one flower you have seen somewhere and visualize it in detail. (Refresh your memory beforehand, if you need to, with a botanical field guide.) Feel the wind in your hair and on your face and hands. Think of the flower as a proud, self-aware being — a living thing without blame or blemish. Look within yourself, as if into a vast landscape, and find that tiny flower.

FLOWING WITH THE STREAM

1 Look at this image of streams meandering among rocks as if you were looking down upon the scene from a high mountain peak. You see the waters swirling around great boulders as they flow in different directions but inexorably bound toward the sea.

2 Think about which element — water or rock — best expresses the essential truth of human life. If we petrify to become a boulder, we will endure. If we dissolve into water, we will flow and endlessly change, until one day we reach the Source.

3 Trace the path of the four streams outward across the rock-strewn landscape. Where the waters crash directly against a rock, there is turbulence. Where the waters yield and "step aside", there is movement — which is the quintessence of life.

If one way be better than another, that,
you may be sure, is nature's way.

ARISTOTLE (384—322 BC)

THE WORLD TREE

WITH ROOTS AROUND THE EARTH AND BRANCHES IN THE HEAVENS, THE WORLD TREE
IS A SYMBOL OF OUR POTENTIAL ASCENT FROM THE PHYSICAL REALM TO THE HIGHER
LEVELS OF THE SPIRIT. THIS MANDALA OFFERS A PARADOXICAL SPIN ON THIS IDEA BY
HAVING THE EARTH'S CORE AS ITS CENTRAL POINT.

1 Look at the basic shape of the mandala — a circle (symbolizing eternity) within a square (symbolizing the created cosmos).

2 Now turn your attention to the tree which connects our Earth with the outer reaches of the universe — the sun and moon are near-neighbours of ours, but the tree's branches stretch to the very limits of eternity, unifying the cosmos in their divine embrace.

3 Contemplate the Earth within the tree's roots. The continent turned toward you is Africa, where great beauty and great poverty and suffering coexist. Extend your love to all the people in need upon this planet.

4 Let go of these imaginings and let your mind penetrate right through to the fiery core of the Earth, the deep inner mystery at the heart of matter. Lose yourself in this mystery.

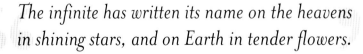

The infinite has written its name on the heavens
in shining stars, and on Earth in tender flowers.

JEAN PAUL RICHTER (1763–1825)

THE UNICORN

THE GREAT AUSTRIAN POET RAINER MARIA RILKE WROTE A SONNET ABOUT THE

UNICORN, BROUGHT INTO EXISTENCE BY OUR OWN BELIEF IN THE CREATURE.

AS A GROUP OF VILLAGERS FED A HORSE WITH THEIR FAITH IN ABSOLUTE PURITY,

A HORN SPROUTED FROM ITS BROW. FAITH MAKES MIRACLES HAPPEN.

1 Look at the border of the mandala — a mixture of natural and man-made elements, like a garden. Our ideal existence on this Earth marries nature with civilization. The cultivation of beauty is akin to the cultivation of the soul.

2 Around the circle's rim, white swallows fly — a glimpse of the miraculous, attainable to all of us who are open to wonder.

3 Now consider the rings within the tree-trunk, marking the passage of years. This is the nature we all live, the gift of our incarnation, fleeting but beautiful.

4 In a forest glade a white horse rears. We sense its strength, its natural perfection. By approaching the horse with selfless admiration, by believing in its purity, we win a priceless trophy: we glimpse the magic horn.

Beyond the pairs of opposites of which the world consists, other, new insights begin.

HERMANN HESSE (1877–1962)

Unicorn quest

A unicorn supposedly appeared to the emperor Huang Di as a token that his reign would be long and peaceful; and another was thought to have brought a gift of jade to the mother of Confucius and laid its head on her lap. Eastern unicorns suggest good omen. Even richer is the medieval Christian tradition by which the unicorn represents purity, or connection with the divine. Although a gentle creature, it could use its horn defensively if needed. You can therefore include the creature in your reflections or meditations as a symbol of your desire to be closer to the spirit. Ask yourself what the horn represents. In other words, what protects you from harm as you pursue your quest for enlightenment?

A QUESTION OF TIME

"To every one of us there must come a time when the whole universe will be found to have been a dream, when we find the soul is infinitely better than its surroundings. It is only a question of time, and time is nothing in the infinite."

SHIRDI SAI BABA (1856–1918)

WHITE WISDOM

"The milk of cows of any colour is white. The sages declare that the milk is wisdom, and that the cows are the sacred scriptures."

UPANISHADS (C.1000 BC)

GOLDEN APPLES

IN GREEK MYTH ONE OF THE TASKS UNDERTAKEN BY THE HERO HERAKLES, OR HERCULES, WAS TO TRAVEL TO THE FAR WEST TO A GARDEN WHERE TWO NYMPHS LIVED. THEY TENDED A TREE BEARING GOLDEN APPLES, GUARDED BY A MANY-HEADED SERPENT. IT WAS HERAKLES' TASK TO KILL THE SERPENT AND STEAL THE APPLES.

1 Imagine the orchard of the Hesperides, the two daughters of Atlas. One of the trees, depicted here, bears golden apples.

2 Trace a route to these apples, then start your journey, inward into the orchard and inward into the self, where all treasures lie.

3 Watching over the apple tree is a many-headed serpent — which you recognize to be an aspect of the self. The only truly dangerous enemies are those that lie within.

4 Look at the demon serpent and summon the qualities you need to banish this monster. You do not need to fight him — only to make him disappear by courageous resolve. Choose an apple from the tree and carry it deep into your inner self. This treasure is deservedly yours. What is it?

The one chased away with a club comes back,
but the one chased away with reason does not.

KIKUYU PROVERB, KENYA

THE SERPENT AND THE EGG

AN EGG SURROUNDED BY A COILED SERPENT WAS A POWERFUL SYMBOL IN THE
ANCIENT GREEK ORPHIC RELIGION, BUT ITS SYMBOLISM IS ESOTERIC. NEVERTHELESS,
THE UNIVERSAL SYMBOLISM OF THE EGG AND SERPENT INDIVIDUALLY MAKES THIS
MYSTERIOUS IMAGE A REWARDING SUBJECT FOR A MANDALA.

1 Look at the four snake-encircled eggs —
symbols of the cosmic serpent protecting the
world. Sense the life-force flowing through
the serpents. Their form suggests the spiralling motion of the cosmos. The egg is consciousness, protected by life itself.

2 Think of egg and serpent in terms of
initiation. Enlightenment is the point at
which spiritual practices break through the
eggshell. This point is within our reach, but
for now we keep both feet on the ground.

3 Contemplate the egg of consciousness
intact within its powerful protection of faith.
Its shell alone is not enough.

4 Look at the serpent eating its own tail —
a celestial circle formed by the earth-bound
creature. Rest your gaze on the central point.

*A song slumbers in all things that lie dreaming on and on and
the world prepares to sing, if you hit upon the magic word.*

JOSEPH FREIHERR VON EICHENDORFF (1788–1857)

LIFE-GIVING SUN

NOTHING IN OUR COSMOS CAN MATCH THE TRANSFORMATIVE POWER OF THE SUN.

IT EVEN PROVIDES US WITH THE MEANS TO SEE. DANGEROUS AT FULL STRENGTH

(LIKE THE GOD ZEUS, WHOM NO MORTAL COULD LOOK UPON WITHOUT SHRIVELLING

TO ASHES), THE SUN IS ALSO PURE LIFE-GIVING ENERGY.

1 Contemplate the frame around the central image of the sun: an elegant pattern such as might be found in a sumptuous palace. Without the sun there would be no art, no civilization.

2 Focus on the central sun image: represented in traditional form as a disk with wavy rays. Understand as you absorb the image into your mind that the sun in its pure essence is beyond sensory experience (except as warmth and light) — in the same way that divinity cannot be comprehended at the sensory level.

3 Let your mind conjure the infinite energy of the sun as you contemplate its symbolic representation. Know that everything you feel derives from this incomprehensible source of love at the centre of our solar system.

The human body is vapour, materialized by sunshine and mixed with the life of the stars.

PARACELSUS (1493–1541)

LOOKING INWARD

"If the eye were not sun-like, it could not see the sun;
if we did not carry within us the very power of God,
how could anything God-like delight us?"

JOHANN WOLFGANG VON GOETHE (1749–1832)

The solar self

Whenever we need to imagine an infinite source of energy, or boundless qualities of any kind, the sun provides us with a perfect symbol, easy to use in meditation. For example, we might choose to imagine ourselves as an endless source of love, spreading over all, bathing

COSMIC CREATION

"That which has no form creates form. That which has no existence brings things into existence."

RUMI (1207–1273)

family, friends, acquaintances and strangers alike in an all-enveloping radiance. No other phenomenon has such connotations of infinite and life-giving abundance. Just as, in several religions, mortals cannot look directly at the godhead, so we are unable grasp the awesome power of the sun. However, we can "visualize" it as an explosion of light and strength; and we have only to look around us, in daylight, to observe how the sun spreads its benefits in all directions. Our own spiritual energies, and our capacity for giving, are no less impressive.

FROG OF GOOD FORTUNE

IN CHINESE FOLKLORE, THE THREE-LEGGED FROG WITH A COIN IN ITS MOUTH IS

RATHER LIKE THE WESTERN SYMBOL OF THE FOUR-LEAFED CLOVER — AN AUGURY OF

GOOD FORTUNE. ALTHOUGH TRADITIONALLY ASSOCIATED WITH A MONETARY WINDFALL,

THE CREATURE IN THIS MEDITATION IS GIVEN A MORE SPIRITUAL DIMENSION.

1 Look at the magic frog — a strange creature that initially we might be inclined to find repellent, even if it were four-legged. Take a minute or so to accept the frog's disability as normal — banish any squeamishness from your mind.

2 Now start to think of the frog as your equal — a being with the right to existence, and to freedom from intolerance.

3 The frog could be eating flies but instead it is making you an offering. You have no wish for money, but perhaps the coin is a symbol of something more meaningful — something your selflessness entitles you to?

4 See the coin as spiritual insight, which is self-rewarding. Focus your eyes on the coin's square centre. Take the coin into your mind, and be at peace.

*I'm a great believer in luck, and I find
the harder I work the more I have of it.*

THOMAS JEFFERSON (1743–1826)

JUST ONE SNOWFLAKE

NOTHING IS MORE LOVELY THAN A SNOWFLAKE. PERFECTLY SYMMETRICAL, WITH A
WONDERFUL DELICACY OF FORM, IT IS ONE OF NATURE'S FINEST ACHIEVEMENTS, NO
LESS SO FOR THE FACT THAT IT IS FLEETING. SIMILARLY, OUR BRIEF LIVES, AND
EPISODES WITHIN THEM, CAN BE BEAUTIFUL FOR ALL THEIR TRANSIENCE.

1 Look at this snowflake. It is complete within itself, and totally unique, even though it is one of millions in a snow shower. Let the thought of the snowflake's singular beauty sink into your mind.

2 Now consider that this is an artificial version of a snowflake, not a real one. You are looking at an image, because the reality of nature can be captured only indistinctly, even when we are out in the fields or woods using all our senses.

3 Move to the centre of this abstract pattern of a snowflake, and meditate on it. Imagine a snow shower is falling outside.

4 Absorb into yourself the yin-yang symbol at the heart of the mandala — the perfect balance of now and then, now and eternity.

He who binds himself to a joy/Does the winged life destroy;/
But he who kisses the moment as it flies/Lives in eternity's sunrise.

WILLIAM BLAKE (1757–1827)

FOOTPRINTS

*"Do not go where the path may lead, go instead
where there is no path and leave a trail."*

RALPH WALDO EMERSON (1803–1882)

The beauty of snow

When snow falls on a landscape, we often see its beauty afresh. The familiar becomes unfamiliar. And, of course, we may find ourselves walking where there are no footprints, enjoying that liberating feeling of being a pioneer of uncharted terrain. Next time you have the

MEETING THE MORNING

"Each soul must meet the morning sun, the new, sweet earth, and the Great Silence alone!"

OHIYESA (1858–1939)

opportunity to go for a walk in the snow, treat it as a walking meditation. Imagine that the landscape is changed, not because it looks different, but because *you* are different. Feel in yourself a freshness of spirit, a restored purity or innocence, that is suitably symbolized in the snow-clad landscape. Your mistakes are erased, and you now have a brand-new page, like a field of snow, on which to write your destiny. Determine to start immediately. Make sure that by the time you finish your walk, you have resolved any difficult dilemmas.

TRANSFORMING FIRE

FIRE IS A MASCULINE, ACTIVE ELEMENT SYMBOLIZING BOTH CREATIVE AND
DESTRUCTIVE ENERGIES. IT CAN SUGGEST PURIFICATION, REGENERATION, OR
REVELATION — AS IN THE BURNING BUSH WITNESSED BY MOSES. THIS MEDITATION
PROGRESSES FROM THE FLAME OF PURIFICATION TO THE FLAME OF INSIGHT.

1 Around the outer circle of the mandala is a ring of small fires you need to pass through to start your meditation. These are the purifying flames you need to bring to emotional attachments to burn them away.

2 The middle ring of bonfires may be seen as a welcome — a celebration that you have purified yourself. Yet there is further work to do, as you must access selflessness. At the deepest level you must be prepared to give love and selfless service. This requires the burning of the ego.

3 Finally you pass into the heart of the mandala — God's "holy fire", as W.B. Yeats called it in his poem "Sailing to Byzantium". You feel an intense heat that does not burn, but rather enlightens — like a great lantern of infinite intensity. You are at peace.

For indeed our God
is a consuming fire.

HEBREWS 12.29

The phoenix

The phoenix is a legendary firebird in ancient Egyptian myth and in other myths of similar derivation. It was a male bird with a blaze of glorious gold and red plumage. After living for five centuries, it would build a nest for itself out of cinnamon twigs, ignite the nest, and thus burn itself to a pile of ashes — out of which a new, young phoenix would emerge. The new phoenix would then deposit the remains (embalmed in a casing of myrrh) in Heliopolis, the City of the Sun. The phoenix later became a symbol of resurrection or immortality. Dwell on this symbolism whenever you seek to make a dramatic change in your life. Think of yourself as the young phoenix, born out of the destruction of bad habits. Imagine the fire from which your new self arises as simultaneously purifying and creative.

THE ESSENTIAL FLAME

*"Just as a candle cannot burn without fire,
men cannot live without a spiritual life."*

THE BUDDHA (C.563—C.460 BC)

CALL OF THE PHOENIX

*"O joy! that in our embers
Is something that doth live."*

WILLIAM WORDSWORTH (1770—1850)

SEASHELLS

AS WELL AS BEING AN AUSPICIOUS LUNAR, FEMININE EMBLEM ASSOCIATED IN

SOME CULTURES WITH FERTILITY AND GOOD FORTUNE, THE SHELL IN ITS OFTEN

COMPLEX INNER GEOMETRY REFLECTS THE MYSTERIOUS DIVINE ORDER THAT

UNDERPINS ALL CREATION.

1 Hold in your mind the border of sea and sand. Think of the waves endlessly breaking and reforming, like the cycles of time itself. Think also of the beach, furrowed by a retreating tide — in the same way, we are marked by the passage of years, while retaining traces of the spirit.

2 Contemplate the long pointed shells shown in cross-section — without their inner geometry, these shells could not inhabit their own elegant form.

3 Finally look at the beautiful double shell in the middle of the mandala. Think of the two spiralling globes as the complementary yin and yang — female and male, stillness and action, compassion and insight. Follow the spirals inward toward the ineffable source of creation, beyond the visible.

Nature never says one thing
and wisdom another.

JUVENAL (C.60–140 AD)

THE LOGIC OF PARADISE

"Sand, sea and sky —
a progression toward the sublime.
Inwardly, unconsciously,
we complete the series: heaven."

LOUISE SOUSTELLE (1911–1962)

Seashore and spirit

The great scientist Sir Isaac Newton, who discovered the laws of motion and the principle of gravity, once likened himself to a boy playing on the seashore, diverting himself by finding a smoother pebble or a prettier shell than usual, while the "great ocean of truth" lay undiscovered

THE OCEAN OF TRUTH

*"If you would swim on the bosom
of the ocean of Truth, you must reduce
yourself to a zero."*

MAHATMA GANDHI (1869—1948)

before him. This image captures vividly our inability to fully comprehend the wonder of creation and of our own existence. Even when we turn our attention from the beach's pebbles and shells to the sea's horizon, we can appreciate the unseen vastness of the ocean only by extrapolating from what we do see — the line where sea meets sky. To intuit the spirit we must start with an awareness of how inadequate even our highest faculties are to receive anything but a dim approximation. Only then can we start to acquire wisdom.

THE COILED SNAKE

THE MOST COMPLEX OF ANIMAL SYMBOLS, THE SNAKE HAS BEEN LINKED VARIOUSLY

WITH FERTILITY, HEALING AND DUPLICITY, AMONG MANY OTHER THEMES. ITS POWER

TO RENEW ITSELF BY SHEDDING ITS SKIN SUGGESTS REJUVENATION, AND IN SOME

EASTERN CULTURES IT IS LINKED WITH THE CREATOR DEITY.

1 Start by looking at the spirals and yin-yang symbols around the edge of the mandala. These denote the rhythms of life, the spiralling motion of the cosmos.

2 Turn to the snake, an image of the life-force, latent with regenerative energy — contrasting with the paved stonework it rests on. Also, the snake is the Other, an intelligence unknowable by the modern mind.

3 Dwell now upon the snake's coiled form. Follow the coil of the body from tail to head, and feel the intensity of its power increasing as you move toward the snake's brain.

4 From the head move your eyes to the ruby, glowing red, around which the snake is coiled. This is the mysterious gift of life itself, a benevolent enigma. Take this truth deep into your mind and relax within its power.

Snakes are the ambassadors of raw nature,
singing songs of mud and fire too solid for the ear.

PEDRO DE HERMANANDEZ (1920–2000)

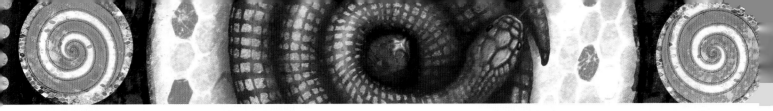

BEYOND THE SENSES

"Our eyes believe themselves, our ears believe other people, our intuition believes the truth of the spirit."

ADAPTED FROM A GERMAN PROVERB

The elusive snake

Snakes dart from shadows into sunlight and back — a mysterious flash of primeval life, making us aware of a primitive force beyond consciousness. Do this simple rainforest meditation to connect yourself with these energies. Sit comfortably, close your eyes and imagine that

THE IMPACT OF NATURE

"When one withdraws all desires as a tortoise withdraws its limbs, then the natural splendour of the world soon manifests itself."

MAHABHARATA (C.400 BC—C.200 AD)

you are in a vast forest. It is daytime but the forest is so deep that no light penetrates here. Imagine you are a tree, and that where your body touches the chair or your clothes, or where your fingers touch each other, these are the points where your leaves encounter the leaves of other trees immediately around you. With your inner eye you sense a snake among your branches — but you do not feel it because touch is felt through your leaves, not your bark. You intuit it as an element of the primordial within yourself. And you sense its hidden power.

FREEING THE WILD SWAN

THE CHAINED SWAN SUGGESTS POWER UNDER THE SUBJUGATION OF REASON —

A TRAVESTY OF WHAT IT MEANS TO BE WILD. IN THIS MEDITATION WE AIM TO FREE

THE BIRD AND RELEASE IT INTO ITS TRUE ELEMENT, AT THE SAME TIME AS WE

RELEASE OUR SPIRIT FROM ITS CONFINING BONDS.

1 Gaze on the feathers within the outer border of this mandala — tokens of the possibility of flight, and reminders that earth is not the only element in which we can live.

2 Now move inward to the two concentric bracelets of interlocking chains. These represent the human world — the imposition of order onto nature. And they also represent the price we pay for such control. Perhaps our dominance over nature can chain our own souls and prevent them from flight.

3 Look at the swan, tamed by humanity. Focus on the radiance of its white-feathered body — infinitely more dazzling than the gold necklace. Imagine that love is pouring from your heart into the creature's wounded soul. In your loving imagination you can release the swan to fly to freedom.

When the swan of the soul takes flight at last,
it needs neither signposts nor maps.

VIJAY BHATTACHARYA (1879–1950)

ASSUMED IDENTITY

*"I will cease to live as a self and will take
as my self my fellow-creatures."*

SHANTIDEVA (C.7TH CENTURY)

LOVE'S WINGS

*"The way to heaven is within. Shake the wings of
love — when love's wings have become strong,
there is no need to trouble about a ladder."*

RUMI (1207–1273)

Swan song

On account of its dazzling white plumage, the swan symbolizes light in many of the world's cultures. It has something of a hermaphrodite nature — suggesting masculine power as well as feminine gracefulness and intuition. These two qualities combine in the Germanic myth of the Valkyrie (warrior goddess) named Kara. Concerned to protect her warrior lover Helgi during a battle, Kara flew over the fighting in her swan's plumage (all Valkyries had the magical ability to appear in swan's form) and sang a song so sublimely soothing, like a lullaby, that the enemy entirely lost their will to fight. In its combination of strength and purity, the swan is not unlike the unicorn, and the creature can be incorporated into your meditations in a similar way (see pages 102–105).

WANDERING TERNS

THE ARCTIC TERN IS A SEABIRD FAMED FOR ITS PRODIGIOUS MIGRATION,

SUMMERING IN THE ARCTIC AND WINTERING IN THE ANTARCTIC TO GIVE ITSELF

MAXIMUM DAYLIGHT IN THE YEAR. THIS MANDALA FOCUSES ON THE IDEA THAT

MOBILITY, AS OPPOSED TO A RIGID OR SEDENTARY NATURE, IS A POSITIVE QUALITY.

1 See the planet Earth at the centre of this mandala as an image of your imagination — a whole world that not even a lifetime's exploration could exhaust. Look beyond the Earth to layers of sky; and then beyond the outer circle of the cosmos, to an unimaginable blankness.

2 Now contemplate the terns on their long-distance migration from pole to pole. Your own imagination can travel even further. It can fly beyond the Earth up through layers of sky and cloud. It can imagine right up to the limits of the unimaginable.

3 Return your concentration to the Earth, and indeed to one spot on the globe in the centre of the mandala. Here in one village, one house, one mind even, is a whole cosmos of richness and value. Just imagine.

Imagination is everything.
It is the preview of life's coming attractions.

ALBERT EINSTEIN (1879–1955)

PERFECT PRAYER

"One single grateful thought raised to heaven is the most perfect prayer."

G.E. LESSING (1729–1781)

Among the doves

There are various ways in which you can use birds in meditations or imaginative exercises. For example, if you ever feel that work, or household chores, or family pressures, have become something of a treadmill, you could visualize yourself as a bird flying high above the

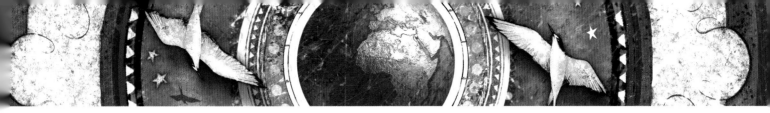

ROOTS AND WINGS

"There are only two lasting benefits we can hope to give to our children. One is roots; the other, wings."

HODDING CARTER (1907–1972)

landscape, looking down upon your life in the overall context of your community. To revitalize your sense of purpose, you might envisage the positive impact your efforts have on those around you. Or alternatively you could create a visualization around the image of the dove, which stands for peace, purity, harmony or love. You might choose to nurture one or more of these qualities in yourself by meditating on the dove that resides within. Or you might instead choose to reflect on the hawk, which lives by the keenness of its perceptions.

A GOLDEN CARP

IN THE EAST THE CARP IS AN OMEN OF GOOD FORTUNE, ESPECIALLY LONG LIFE, ON ACCOUNT OF THE FISH'S OWN LONGEVITY. IT WAS ALSO GIVEN IN EMBLEMATIC FORM TO STUDENTS WITH WISHES FOR SUCCESS IN EXAMINATIONS. THE CARP IN ITS POND CAN BE LIKENED TO INSIGHT — A DISTINCT GLEAM IN THE MURKY DEPTHS.

1 Look at the overhead view of the pond represented in this mandala. Start with the raked gravel surround, symbolizing the flow of time. Then move to the pond's edge — although a man-made artefact, this takes the form of a circle, denoting our yearning for a glimpse of spiritual perfection, of eternity.

2 Gaze at the various living things in and around the pond: the butterflies, dragonflies and waterlilies. Look too at the fallen leaves, which remind us of the inevitability of decay in nature's grand cycle.

3 Pick out the subtle gleam of the carp, just visible in the inky waters. This may be our own good fortune, which habitual preoccupations often prevent us from seeing. Perhaps the carp is a dawning insight — a gratefulness that we are part of nature.

The eye of the silent heart will see into great depths,
and the ear of the silent mind will hear untold wonders.

ST HESYCHIUS OF JERUSALEM (5TH CENTURY AD)

SCALLOP SHELLS

LIKE OTHER KINDS OF SHELL, THE SCALLOP DENOTES FERTILITY AND FEMININITY,

THANKS TO ITS ASSOCIATION WITH WATER. THE FACT THAT OYSTERS CONTAIN PEARLS

GAVE RISE TO THE MYTH OF APHRODITE BEING BORN OUT OF A SHELL, DEPICTED BY

THE ITALIAN RENAISSANCE PAINTER SANDRO BOTTICELLI AS A SCALLOP.

1   Look at the wave forms in the corners of this mandala and within the circle that immediately surrounds the central scallop shell. Think of the ocean rising and falling in its tidal rhythms determined by the moon, symbol of eternal change.

2   Turn your attention to the outer circle of scallops framing the larger, central shell. Think of nature producing near-identical forms from the genetic blueprint of a species. The self is central, but in fact there are countless selves, all participating in the unified cosmos.

3   Move in your mind through the successive circles of the image, dwelling on each circular band in turn. Finally, let your eye rest on the central shell — the perfect moment within its framework of endless change.

Peace is the one–way flow of time without
any ripple of regret or resistance.

MARIE LE STRANGE (1890–1976)

THE PILGRIM'S PATH

*"Life can only be understood backwards;
but it must be lived forwards."*

SØREN KIERKEGAARD (1813–1855)

WAY BACK

*"Reverse time's arrow and make it your signpost.
Revisit your old haunts and feel the years wither and
drop from your limbs, heart and brain."*

SAMUEL HAROLDSON (1912–1990)

The pilgrim salmon

In medieval Europe the scallop shell was the badge of pilgrims. In the animal world there is no more impressive pilgrim than the Atlantic salmon, which reaches maturity in the ocean and then travels thousands of miles to the up-river streams where it first saw the light of day, itself to spawn. The idea of retracing our steps to a place of origin is an appealing one. You might consider constructing a meditation on this idea — for example, one that takes you back to a phase in your life when you felt especially happy, and involves bringing some image or visualized object back with you from that period, like a time traveller; and then using this as a totem to renew your energies or your resolve. Or you might like to go on an actual pilgrimage to a wood or other place of nature where you felt happy as a child, and meditate there.

GAZING AT THE TIGER

ANIMALS HAVE AN INTENSE MYSTERY ABOUT THEM. WE MAY BE AT A LOSS TO

UNDERSTAND THE MENTALITY OF SOMEONE WHO SPEAKS A DIFFERENT LANGUAGE

FROM OUR OWN, YET AN ANIMAL'S CONSCIOUSNESS IS EVEN MORE BAFFLING. THIS

PUZZLEMENT SHADES INTO AWE, WHICH, DEPRIVED OF ANY FEAR, BRINGS INSIGHTS.

1 With your eyes move slowly from the outer edge of the mandala toward the centre. Imagine first that you are entering the jungle, then a reserve within that jungle where wild tigers roam. You see four of them from a safe distance; and closer to the heart of the reserve you see four tiger footprints.

2 Now prepare for a closer encounter with a tiger by meditating on the Greek cross within a circle within a square — a miniature mandala in itself, suggestive of spirit (circle), the natural world (square), and the incarnation of spirit in creation (cross).

3 You are now given the privilege to come close to the tiger and look right into its eye. You lose yourself in its mystery, safe in the knowledge that your spiritual awareness protects you from any real danger.

*Humankind differs from the animals only by
a little, and most people throw that away.*

CONFUCIUS (551—479 BC)

A BIRD'S EGG

THE EGG IS A UNIVERSAL SYMBOL OF BEGINNINGS, WHOSE FRAGILITY EMPHASIZES HOW PRECIOUS IT IS. AS WITH MANY DIFFERENT KINDS OF PROJECT, CONDITIONS MUST BE RIGHT FOR THE BREAKTHROUGH TO TAKE PLACE. NURTURING IS A NECESSARY PRELIMINARY TO FULFILMENT.

1 Look at the border around the egg, with its delicate leaves. These symbolize the preparation that any serious project of self-fulfilment or self-analysis, or any major new direction in life, requires. Trace the interwoven lines of the border as a symbolic gesture of readiness to acquire fresh insights.

2 Progress now to the egg itself, sitting on its intricately woven nest. Sense within the shell the new life pulsing with potential. Send out love from your heart to wrap the egg in a force-field of nurturing warmth.

3 Think for a moment of the change you would like to see — whether in yourself, or your family or friends, or your community. Bring the image of the egg deep into your consciousness, and imagine it getting ready to hatch. Finally, it does so. There is new life.

Everything in nature contains all the power of nature.
Everything is made of one hidden stuff.

RALPH WALDO EMERSON (1803–1882)

GATEWAY OF CHANGE

*"When the way comes to an end, then change —
having changed, you pass through."*

I CHING (12TH CENTURY BC)

Life cycles

Any animal whose life cycle has distinct stages — a bird, a butterfly, a frog — may be used as a template for meditation to prepare yourself for a life change of some kind, as described on page 149. Birds have three distinct stages: the egg; the juvenile, which must learn to fly and

A DREAM OF FLIGHT

"The soul stirs within its chrysalis, dreaming that it will one day be an angel. It will."

LOU ANDREAS-SALOMÉ (1861–1937)

feed itself; and the adult, which may or may not migrate. The butterfly is a useful image because the emergence of the adult from the chrysalis is beautiful and enabling. You could also meditate around a frog's life cycle, because a creature confined to water (the tadpole) acquires the ability to move on land. Then there is the chameleon, which protects itself by changing its appearance to match its surroundings. Which of these creatures you build into your meditations on change is entirely, of course, a matter of personal preference.

THE BUSINESS OF BEES

THE BEEHIVE IS AN IMAGE OF COOPERATIVE ENDEAVOUR WITHIN A SOCIETY. THIS

IDEA IS ENRICHED BY A SPIRITUAL SYMBOLISM ATTACHED TO THE INDIVIDUAL BEE,

IN ITS CONVERSION OF NECTAR TO HONEY. NOT SURPRISINGLY, THE BEEHIVE HAS

BEEN SEEN AS A MODEL FOR MONASTIC COMMUNITIES.

1 Look at the two concentric circles, symbolizing spirituality, and the square between them, denoting the created cosmos, which is also suggested by the various flowers.

2 Let your eyes rest in turn on the eight bees within the outer circle. Bees are emblematic of the soul, and hence participate in the spirituality that both circles of the mandala represent.

3 Pass into the inner circle (the hive, with its honeycomb), and rest your eyes on one of the bees that has filled the comb with honey. Think of the comb as your mind, and the honey as your awareness of the divine.

4 Take the mandala as a whole deep into your mind. Let the image of the hive fill your consciousness. Feel connected to the world community of the spirit.

No one drop of honey can claim to be from the nectar of a single flower. All creatures are one but do not realize this.

UPANISHADS (C.1000 BC)

DWELLING IN PEACE

"Better a dry morsel with quiet than a house full of feasting with strife."

PROVERBS 107.1

The worry hive

The image of the beehive can be used in a very straight-forward visualization to reduce levels of everyday stress. If you are troubled by a constant background noise of vague anxiety, then find a quiet place to sit, close your eyes, take a few deep breaths and start to envisage all

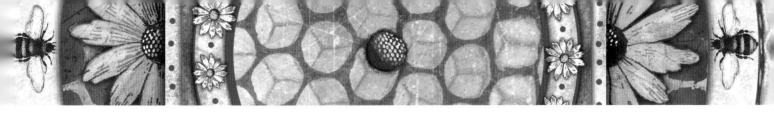

LET THOUGHTS PASS

"Thoughts of themselves have no substance; let them arise and pass away unheeded. Thoughts will not take form of themselves, unless they are grasped by the attention; if they are ignored, there will be no appearing and no disappearing."

ASHVAGHOSHA (1ST CENTURY AD)

your problems as a swarm of bees buzzing around your head. In your mind's eye conjure up a beehive just in front of you. Then mentally guide the bees one by one safely into the hive. With each bee that is brought home, the buzzing becomes a little quieter, until it finally ceases altogether. Your anxieties — even the ones that are nameless — have been shepherded away to a place where they cannot cause you any trouble. At least for a while, you are at peace with yourself. Remember this feeling next time stresses start to trouble you.

EYES OF THE PEACOCK

THE COSMOS HAS AN INTRINSIC RADIANCE THAT IS NOT ALWAYS APPARENT:

WE CAN BE DISTRACTED FROM BEAUTY AND WONDER BY OUR VARIOUS HUMAN

PREOCCUPATIONS — FOR EXAMPLE, WORK OR EMOTIONS. THE PEACOCK IS AN IMAGE

OF REVELATION, USED IN THIS MANDALA TO OPEN THE EYELID OF AWARENESS.

1 Start by looking at the outer circle of the mandala — symbol of eternity or spirit. Along the circumference are iridescent "eye" motifs of a peacock's tail. Could these have some connection, in their beauty, with the eternal?

2 Contemplate each concentric band of the mandala in turn. Dwell on the miracle of colour and pattern, and the vision that allows us so vividly to perceive it.

3 Now gaze at the triangle within the mandala — a symbol of both harmony and, in alchemy, fire. Feather and fire coexist in a harmonious universe.

4 Lastly, dwell on the peacock itself. Life is beautifully, pricelessly evanescent, like the flash of a peacock's tail. Its perfection may be hidden, but the enlightened soul will see this glory — a wonderful gift from the One.

Dive deep, O mind, in the ocean of God's beauty! If you descend to the utmost depths, there you will find the gem of love.

BENGALI HYMN

FURTHER READING

The following is a brief guide to books on meditation, mandalas and nature, as well as a few books of more general interest.

Bucknell, R. and Kang, C. (ed.) *The Meditative Way*. RoutledgeCurzon, Richmond (UK), 1997.

Coogan, M.D. (ed.) *World Religions*. Duncan Baird Publishers, London, 1998; Oxford University Press, New York, 1998.

Eastcott, M. J. *Silent Path*. Rider, London, 1969; new edition Rider, London, 1989.

Emerson, R.W. *The Essential Writings of Ralph Waldo Emerson*. Random House (Modern Library Classics), New York, 2000.

Fontana, D. *The Meditator's Handbook*. Element Books, Shaftesbury (UK) and Boston (Mass.), 1992; new edition Thorsons, London, 2002.

Fontana, D. *Learn to Meditate: The Art of Tranquillity, Self-Awareness and Insight*. Duncan Baird Publishers, London, 1998; Chronicle Books, San Francisco, 1999.

Fontana, D. *Meditation Week by Week*. Duncan Baird Publishers, London, 2004.

Fontana, D. *Meditating with Mandalas*. Duncan Baird Publishers, London, 2005.

Gawain, S. *Creative Visualization*. Bantam Books, New York, 1982.

Hageneder, F. *The Living Wisdom of Trees*. Duncan Baird Publishers, London, 2005; Chronicle Books, San Francisco, 2005.

Kear, K. *Flower Wisdom*. Thorsons, London, 2000.

Lao Tzu. *Tao Te Ching*. Hackett, Indianapolis (Ind.), 1993.

LeShan, L. *How to Meditate*. Turnstone, London 1983; Little, Brown & Co., New York, 1999.

Levering, M. *Zen Inspirations*. Duncan Baird Publishers, London, 2004.

McDonald, K. *How to Meditate: A Practical Guide*. Wisdom Publications, New York, 1995.

Palmer, J.D. *Animal Wisdom*, Thorsons, London, 2001.

Tenzin-Dolma, L. *Understanding the Planetary Myths*. Foulsham, Slough (UK), 2004.

Thoreau, H.D. *Walden*. Oxford University Press, Oxford, 1995; Yale University Press, New Haven (Conn.), 2004.

Tresidder, J. (ed.) *The Complete Dictionary of Symbols*. Duncan Baird Publishers, London, 2004; Chronicle Books, San Francisco, 2004.

Tucci, G. *The Theory and Practice of the Mandala*. Rider, London, 1969; new edition Dover Publications, New York, 2001.

GENERAL INDEX

For ease of reference, this index has been divided into two parts: the first is an index to concepts that occur throughout the book; the second is an index of specific symbols.

Entries in *italic* type refer to captions to photographs. Entries in **bold** type indicate symbols that are included in the title of the mandala.

INDEX TO SYMBOLS

ACKNOWLEDGMENTS

The publisher would like to thank the following people, museums, and photographic libraries for permission to reproduce their material. Every care has been taken to trace copyright holders. However, if we have omitted anyone we apologize and will, if informed, make corrections to any future edition. **PICTURE CREDITS: Page 8** Getty Images/ National Geographic/Joel Sartore; **17** Corbis/ Steve Terrill; **21** Corbis/Jason Hawkes; **31** Corbis/Geray Sweeney; **47** NHPA/Daniel Heuclin. **TEXT CREDITS: Pages 90–91** haiku from *The Penguin Book of Zen Poetry* ed. and trans. Lucien Stryk and Takashi Ikemoto (Penguin, 1981), reproduced by permission of Lucien Stryk.